Oxfordshire A very Classic Location

Oxford is like no other city in the world. Its global prominence and reputation attracts over 7 million visitors to the city a year alone. Its architectural elegance and iconic university buildings of golden stone make it a stunning city to explore for a weekend break or longer. It is home to historic treasures that are renowned as the oldest, finest and very often the only ones of their kind.

Alongside the famous "dreaming spires," visitors discover that Oxford is a vibrant, contemporary city that feels as good as it looks. Oxford is simply buzzing with chic restaurants, bistros and bars, traditional pubs and attractions, and a lively and ever-growing cultural scene that has earned the coveted title of Centre of Culture until 2008.

Beyond the city, Oxford's central location offers a gateway to a wealth of glorious countryside and attractions.

Visit Oxford is delighted to sponsor Classic Locations Oxfordshire, which truly reflects the diversity of choice and hidden highlights of this remarkable city and its surroundings, for both residents and visitors alike.

Suzanne Lockhart
Tourism Officer
Oxford City Counci

www.visitoxford.org

judi dench   jim broadbent   kate winsle

Oxfordshire A county of surprises

Oxfordshire is a county full of surprises and beauty. It is home to hundreds of accomplished artists and writers. The mix of highly talented individuals and both new and well-established organisations – galleries, museums, libraries, theatres, music groups, orchestras and festivals of great variety – all contribute to a diverse and abundant cultural life.

Oxford Inspires is the cultural development agency for Oxfordshire. It is part of our role to encourage residents, students and visitors to discover and enjoy more of the city and county.

And there is much more to Oxford and Oxfordshire than is suggested by the images of punts, towers and spires that are now seen all over the world. Taking time fully to explore the city and the county is time exceptionally well spent.

I welcome Classic Locations Oxfordshire because it shares with visitors to the county the cultural "insider knowledge" that will make their stay here much more rewarding. At the same time, it will enable people who already live in Oxfordshire to discover new facets of a place they thought they knew well.

Robert Hutchison
Chief Executive
Oxford Inspires

Oxford Inspires
Cultural action in Oxfordshire

Contents

QVOD FELICITER VORTAT
ACADEMICI OXONIENS
BIBLIOTHECAM HANC
VOBIS REIPVBLICAEQVE
LITERATORVM
T. B. P.

A quick guide Oxford

Where's the university?	"Oxford University" is in fact 39 colleges spread throughout the city. The majority however are all fairly central, and within walking distance of each other.
The old bit	A circuit of St Giles, Broad Street, Holywell Street, Longwall Street, High Street and Cornmarket Street. Includes many of the colleges, plus Blackwell's Bookshop, Sheldonian Theatre, Radcliffe Camera, Bodleian Library and Botanic Garden.
The new bit	The Oxford Castle area has been redeveloped into a trendy mix of hotels, bars, restaurants and apartments.
The bit in the middle	Oxford still seems to be working on that. George Street is fast-food and club heaven, if that's what you like. The area towards the railway station could politely be described as a little run down. The Westgate Centre needs blowing up.
Out of town	The slightly bohemian suburb of Jericho, a brisk walk from the end of Beaumont Street, contains some excellent restaurants and shops.
	Cowley Road is home to Oxford's carnival and some of its best ethnic restaurants and shops.
	Summertown, on Banbury Road, is a residential suburb served by a wide range of restaurants, shops and galleries.
Getting in	Oxford has major parking problems. Use the Park & Ride, or park in the Gloucester Green or Westgate multi-storeys and walk around.
Getting around	Start with the open-top bus tour to get your bearings - www.citysightseeingoxford.com
Background	The Oxford Story for a potted history of the city - www.oxfordstory.co.uk
Events	Artweeks, Cowley Road Carnival, Oxford Literary Festival, hundreds of music and arts events. The Oxford Science Festival at Science Oxford is suitable for all ages. There's a wide range of activities from debates, lectures, networking events, exhibitions, hands-on activities and performances: a real opportunity to find out how science impacts on what goes on around us.
Tourist information	15-16 Broad Street Oxford OX1 3AS ✆ 01865 726871 www.visitoxford.org

LOCATION SCOUTS: PAUL ROUSE, GORDON BEACH

◀ THE MANY FACES OF OXFORD

Quod Oxford

Gossip & Secrets

The food	Contemporary English with a definite Italian influence.
The drink	Wide selection of reasonably priced wines, spirits and cocktails.
Why is it so good?	Lovely environment – modern décor in an old Georgian banking hall, with large pieces of modern art adorning the walls.
Why is it not so good?	Service can be slow at busy times. Can be very busy around graduation time.
To die for	Warm chicken salad with roasted vegetables – delicious!
Occasions	Business lunch or meal with family.
When to go	Nice days to enjoy the terrace area.
Atmosphere	Bustling.
In the know	House wine is surprisingly drinkable.

Essentials

Run by	Part of Mogford Group, who own the Old Parsonage and Gee's.
Where is it?	High Street, across from Radcliffe Square.
How much?	Average starter £4-£7, main courses around £10, puddings £4-£5.
When is it open?	Daily, 12 noon till 11pm.
Get in touch	92-94 High Street Oxford OX1 4BN ✆ 01865 202505 www.quod.co.uk

LOCATION SCOUT: SUZANNE LOCKHART

Chiang Mai Oxford

Gossip & Secrets

The food	Thai restaurant with a fantastic range of fish, curries and vegetarian dishes in addition to the usual favourites.
The drink	Reasonably priced wine, plus Singha beer in small or large size.
Why is it so good?	Fantastic food, great service and a warm atmosphere set in an amazing 17th century building. Have never had a bad meal here.
Why is it not so good?	Gets booked up easily. Recommend booking at the beginning of the week for a weekend night.
To die for	My husband says that their Tom Ka Gai (chicken and coconut soup) beats any that he has had in Thailand! For me, the steamed fish is amazingly good, with fantastic flavours.
Occasions	Ideal for a romantic evening or with a small group of friends.
When to go	Busy most evenings! 6.30-7pm is a nice time to come for a relaxed meal, or later for a buzzy atmosphere.
Atmosphere	Busy but friendly. Children welcomed.
In the know	The stairs upstairs are quite steep, so book a table downstairs if any of your group are elderly. Stilettos are also a no-no as the steps are quite slippery (I'm speaking from experience!).

Essentials

How big?	Two floors, with a total of 66 covers.
Where is it?	Down a small passageway at the top of the High Street in Oxford (next to White Stuff). Easy to miss. Park in Westgate shopping centre or on the High Street after 6.30pm.
How much?	Average starter – £6.50 Average main – £8.50. Lunch – average £7.00
When is it open?	Seven days a week: Lunchtime from 12-2.30pm, evenings from 6-10.30pm (last food orders). 10pm last orders on Sundays.
Get in touch	Kemp Hall Passage 130a High Street Oxford OX1 5DH ✆ 01865 202233 www.chiangmaikitchen.co.uk

LOCATION SCOUT: KATHRYN SMITH

Holywell's Bar & Brasserie Oxford

Gossip & Secrets

The food	Excellent grills, vegetarian dishes and Fish of the Day specials.
The drink	Range of good quality wines, reasonably priced. Good selection of draught beers including Youngs.
Why is it so good?	Very friendly staff who obviously love working there: they always seem to make time to spend with customers, even when busy. Food is very reasonably priced with very generous portions.
Why is it not so good?	Can get very crowded during term time.
To die for	Holywells Sundae: vanilla, chocolate & toffee ice cream topped with chocolate Brownies, warm chocolate sauce and cream!
Occasions	Perfect for a drink with friends after work, evening meal, light lunch, business lunches, to celebrate or for a great night out.
When to go	Need to book on Friday and Saturday nights.
Atmosphere	This versatile venue is split level, spread over three floors built around a stunning feature octagon glass structure. Creatively lit with a small outdoor-decked drinking area. Lots of scrubbed wood and laminated veneer floors, traditional furniture. Modern decor completes its sophisticated, welcoming and relaxing ambience.
In the know	On the ground floor: a romantically-lit area to enjoy a pre-dinner drink or relax after dinner on comfy leather sofas with your coffee.

Essentials

How big?	60 Covers
Where is it?	Formerly called Next Door. Situated at the end of Broad Street next to the Kings Arms.
How much?	Average starter £4.95; mains £12.95; dessert £4.75. Monday to Thursday: three course meal includes a bottle of Sauvignon Blanc or Merlot — £30 for two plus service.
When is it open?	Lunch and evenings seven days a week.
Get in touch	38 Holywell Street Oxford OX1 3SP ☎ 01865 203536 www.holywells.net

LOCATION SCOUT: ALISON PETRASH

News Cafe Oxford

Gossip & Secrets

The food	Good range of meals and snacks. Serves good old English food, sometimes with a twist!
The drink	Great list of juices and fruit smoothies, plus an extensive range of teas. They do sell wine but the choice is very limited.
Why is it so good?	On a busy Saturday in the summer it can be a haven from the tourists – it's mainly locals who go there.
Why is it not so good?	Can get very busy at lunchtimes, when you have to be ordering food to get a table.
To die for	Local Minted Lamb Burgers with Black Pepper Mayo and Chunky Fries always hits the spot!
Occasions	Great pit stop while shopping. Lots of small, intimate tables just right for a chat with a friend.
When to go	Early morning on a weekend – they do a great range of cooked breakfasts.
Atmosphere	A real Oxford atmosphere – lots of newspapers to read, posters of local events and local adverts. Relaxed and yet it has a certain buzz.

Essentials

Where is it?	Tucked away off Cornmarket Street, just past Waterstone's.
How much?	Starters £4; main £8.50, dessert £3.60.
Get in touch	1 Ship Street Oxford OX1 3DA ✆ 01865 242317

LOCATION SCOUT: JILL TRELOGGEN

G&D's Oxford

Gossip & Secrets

The food	Mainly ice cream, but also great bagels and cakes.
The drink	Coffees, milkshakes, ice cream shakes.
Why is it so good?	Best ice-cream in Oxford. Freshly made in the basement of the shop, with locally-produced Jersey cream and no added ingredients.
Why is it not so good?	Can be too crowded.
To die for	After Eight Ice Cream.
Occasions	That sweet kick after a meal or a hot day.
Atmosphere	Cheery and laid-back.
In the know	Opens at 8am for that early coffee or breakfast.
Don't just take our word for it	The queues out the door at 11pm at night show how popular it is!

Essentials

Run by	George and his dog! (G&D's)
How big?	Approx 15 covers
Where is it?	Opposite Duke of Cambridge, on Little Clarendon Street.
How much?	Around £2.50 for a cone.
When is it open?	8am-12 midnight daily.
Get in touch	2 Dartington House Little Clarendon Street Oxford OX1 2HS ✆ 01865 516652

LOCATION SCOUT: SUZANNE LOCKHART

Porters Oxford

Gossip & Secrets

The food	Brassiere style food, good quality and good value.
The drink	Anything from coffee to cocktails.
Why is it so good?	A lovely relaxed, friendly atmosphere as soon as you walk in.
Why is it not so good?	Portions on the small side, but more than adequate.
To die for	Apple crumble, but not as you know it. The two halves of an apple are scraped out and refilled with a crumble topping ....mmm.
Occasions	Night out with friends or a meal for two.
When to go	Anytime really. At its busiest on Fridays and Saturdays.
Atmosphere	Relaxed, friendly, welcoming.
In the know	You can book private parties and use the upstairs room.

Essentials

Run by	Jon Flint and Sara Reevell.
How big?	Can seat 40 downstairs and another 80 upstairs.
Where is it?	Set on the corner of Little Clarendon Street, just off Woodstock Road, close to St Giles.
How much?	Average starter £4, main course £10, dessert £4.
When is it open?	Lunch and evenings 7 days a week.
Get in touch	1-2 Little Clarendon Street Oxford OX1 2HP
	✆ 01865 511442

LOCATION SCOUT: CLAIRE WILLCOX

Branca Oxford

Gossip & Secrets

The food	Honest, gutsy Italian food with flair.
The drink	Well-chosen quality wine and sophisticated cocktails. Good beer, always cold!
Why is it so good?	Impressively large dining area with a stunning interior which feels informal and inviting.
To die for	The smoked haddock and parsley risotto is an out of this world experience, as is the linguine with tiger prawns, chilli and lemon.
Occasions	Great for romantic dinners or larger occasions.
When to go	Anytime.
Atmosphere	Warm and sophisticated.
In the know	Lunch special for £5.95, available from 12.00 to 5pm! Includes glass of wine or beer.
Don't just take our word for it	Michelin listed – one of only four stand-alone restaurants in Oxford.

Essentials

Run by	Paul Petrillo
How big?	110 seats
Where is it?	Walton Street, one of the most popular areas for dining in Oxford.
How much?	Early supper, Monday to Friday 5-7pm: £10 for two courses.
When is it open?	11am to 11pm every day.
Get in touch	111 Walton Street Oxford OX2 6AJ
	✆ 01865 556111
	www.branca-restaurants.com

LOCATION SCOUT: AMANDA WYATT

Taste Oxford

Gossip & Secrets

The food	Modern and minimalist listed under "from the air, land, water and heaven." Formerly known as Sip.
The drink	Expensive, but unique cocktails and bottled beers.
Why is it so good?	Staff are friendly and layout is stunning.
Why is it not so good?	Expensive. Drinks can take a long time to prepare.
To die for	Tempura chicken.
Occasions	Business lunch or drinks with the girls.
When to go	Friday or Saturday nights – can be quiet on other nights.
Atmosphere	Exclusive and chilled.
In the know	Sunday barbecues on nice days, out the back.
Don't just take our word for it	It is the in-place for wealthy students

Essentials

How big?	Approx 40 covers
Where is it?	Opposite Le Petit Blanc on Walton Street.
How much?	Average starter £4-7, main courses around £10, puddings £4-5.
When is it open?	Daily, lunch and dinner.
Get in touch	102 Walton Street Oxford OX2 6EB
	✆ 01865 311322

LOCATION SCOUT: SUZANNE LOCKHART

Bombay Oxford

Gossip & Secrets

The food	Officially entitled Bangladeshi halal cuisine, including balti, curry and tandoori.
The drink	BYO — but lots of local shops selling alcohol nearby.
Why is it so good?	Best Indian restaurant in Oxford by far: relaxed feel, staff very friendly and efficient. A real community restaurant with lots of recognisable regulars (including me!).
Why is it not so good?	Can be rather busy at weekends with large groups of people, particularly during term-time.
To die for	Shahi Korma or Chicken Jalfrezi.
Occasions	Relaxed informal meal for 2 or 20!
When to go	Not at 8pm on a Saturday night — unless you have booked.
Atmosphere	Relaxed and enjoyable.
In the know	When you order a take-away they throw in lots of extras, so don't over-order.
Don't just take our word for it	Numerous awards and accolades adorn the walls, including Harden's.

Essentials

How big?	52 covers
Where is it?	Far end (ie away from the city centre) of Walton Street, near the Victoria pub.
How much?	Average starter £4, main course £9.
When is it open?	7 days a week — lunch and evenings, including bank holidays.
Get in touch	82 Walton Street Oxford OX2 6EA ✆ 01865 511188

LOCATION SCOUT: SUZANNE LOCKHART

Le Petit Blanc Oxford

Gossip & Secrets

The food	Simple, wholesome, modern take on French cuisine, with recipes developed by Raymond Blanc.
The drink	Excellent selection of wines – over 40, mainly French of course!
Why is it so good?	Terrific food, consistent quality, efficient and friendly staff.
Why is it not so good?	Can be a bit antiseptic if quiet.
To die for	Herb pancakes with Gruyere, ham, mushrooms and kirsch (£9.50).
Occasions	Great for couples or groups. Private dining room seats 14.
When to go	Lunchtime for a shopper's break, or early evening, pre-theatre.
Atmosphere	Décor is ultra-modern to the point of minimalist. Great buzz when busy, but a little stark during quieter moments. Great art on walls.
In the know	The Prix Fixe menu is excellent value – £12 for two courses, £14.50 for three. Available from 12pm-7pm and 10pm-11pm for night owls. Good children's menu.
Don't just take our word for it	Two AA rosettes. Bib Gourmand from Michelin.

Essentials

How big?	120 covers.
Where is it?	Top end (away from town) of Walton Street, in trendy Jericho.
How much?	Starters – £4.50 to £7.50 Mains – £9.50 to £17.95 Desserts – £4.50 to £7.75 House wine from £12.95. Good selection in the £15-£20 range.
When is it open?	12pm to 11pm (last serving) daily.
Get in touch	71- 72 Walton Street Oxford OX2 6AG ✆ 01865 510999 www.lepetitblanc.co.uk

LOCATION SCOUT: PAUL ROUSE

Al Shami Oxford

Gossip & Secrets

The food	Homemade Lebanese food, simply served and superbly fresh.
The drink	Some good vintages of Chateau Musar - choose as old a vintage as possible to have a wonderfully rounded and surprisingly good wine.
Why is it so good?	Like being on Mediterranean holiday for a night.
Why is it not so good?	Parking is a nightmare in Jericho - walk if at all possible.
To die for	Wonderful appetisers and super sticky Lebanese sweets to accompany thick coffee or mint tea.
Occasions	Has a private dining room for a fun, hands-on food sharing experience with friends.
When to go	Equally good at lunch or dinner.
Atmosphere	White-washed Lebanese décor. Busy but not frantic.
In the know	Ask the waiter to recommend a selection of starters and mains.

Essentials

How big?	Restaurant 40 covers, private dining 50.
Where is it?	On the apex of Walton Crescent and Richmond Road in Jericho.
How much?	Appetisers from £1.80 to £4.00. Main courses from £6.50 to £12.00. Sweets from £1.50 to £3.00. They will select a menu for you from £15.00 per person.
When is it open?	Noon to midnight.
Get in touch	25 Walton Crescent Oxford OX1 2JG ✆ 01865 310066 www.al-shami.co.uk

LOCATION SCOUT: TOM LEWIS

Gossip & Secrets

The food	Fries, tapas and nachos – but only as accompaniments.
The drink	What they're the best at: fantastic cocktails made from fresh fruit.
Why is it so good?	Friendly, knowledgeable staff, fantastic cocktails, and the best selection of spirits in Oxford – over 40 vodkas, 30 Bourbons, 11 gins…
Why is it not so good?	Gets quite crowded at weekends and can be noisy.
To die for	The cocktails! Amazing combinations using only fruit. The full time barristas will create special cocktails for you based on your needs (like a sore throat!).
Occasions	Perfect for a girls night out.
When to go	Any night. At weekends, get there by 7.30 – 8pm to get a table.
Atmosphere	Funky, trendy, pretty laid back.
In the know	Go early and get a table downstairs where you can request table service before it gets busy.
Don't just take our word for it	Consistently comes 2nd in national competitions for best bartender and best cocktail bar, losing only to the big, over hyped London bars.

Essentials

Run by	Matt Davies – the owner.
How big?	2 floors. 110 capacity in total.
Where is it?	Walton Street in trendy Jericho – towards the city centre end.
How much?	Wine from £2.70 a glass, beer £2.80
	Average cocktail £5.50, shooters £3 for two.
When is it open?	Sun – Thurs 4-12pm, Fri & Sat 4pm-1am.
Get in touch	32 Walton Street
	Oxford OX2 6AA
	✆ 01865 553732
	www.raoulsbar.com

LOCATION SCOUT: KATHRYN SMITH

Gee's Oxford

Gossip & Secrets

The food	Some of the best food in Oxford. Specialising in local produce where possible, the menu changes to reflect the seasons.
The drink	Great wine list. They use Milton Sandford Wines who supply wines sourced directly from vineyards. Plus: join the Gee's wine club.
Why is it so good?	A Victorian conservatory that used to be a florist and greengrocers. The setting is perfect and the service is wonderful.
Why is it not so good?	This Oxford Institution is a big celebration place for graduating students, so lunches can sometimes be a bit of a scrum.
To die for	The fish. Flown in daily from Jersey, it still tastes of the sea.
Occasions	Romantic dinners, graduations (!), leisurely lunches and any other occasion you can make an excuse for.
When to go	Sunday evening jazz – but book. Sunny days when you can sit outside and watch the world go by.
Atmosphere	Relaxed chic, but still posh enough to impress.
In the know	The manager's brother is the fisherman in Jersey.
Don't just take our word for it	The Times named it one of the top ten best places for Sunday lunch.

Essentials

How big?	Restaurant – 85; terrace – 40.
Where is it?	20 minute walk along the Banbury Road from St Giles.
How much?	Starters average £6-8; mains £15; puddings £6. Two-course set lunch £12.95; Star dishes each week – £25. House wine £10.50.
Get in touch	61 Banbury Road Oxford OX2 6PE ✆ 01865 553540 www.gees-restaurant.co.uk

LOCATION SCOUT: KATE ROUSE

The Lemon Tree Oxford

Gossip & Secrets

The food	Modern, trendy menu that changes with seasonal tweaks. Good salads and very good value 2 or 3 course lunch menu.
The drink	Extensive wine list that hits most spots, plus good cocktails. Try the delicious Lemon Tree Martini with a Lemoncello-washed glass filled with lemon vodka. The front of the restaurant is a great bar.
Why is it so good?	One of Oxford's old favourites. Having established it before selling it, original owner Clinton Pugh bought it back, rescuing it from interim mediocrity. Now very popular and very fashionable again.
Why is it not so good?	The food can be a little inconsistent, but the venue is fabulous, so you forgive it!
To die for	The Mediterranean décor, a cross between Andalucia and Morocco. Gorgeous palms and a lovely garden for the summer.
Occasions	Relaxing lunches or dinners.
When to go	Not for lunch Monday – Wednesday.
Atmosphere	Sophisticated Mediterranean dining.
In the know	The owner lives some of the time in Spain, hence the strong Moorish influence on decor.

Essentials

Run by	Clinton Pugh.
Where is it?	About a mile out of the city on the Woodstock Road. Small car park at rear.
How much?	Average starters £5-6; mains £15; desserts £5.50. 2 course lunch £10.95; 3 courses £12.95. Cocktails average £6, Champagne by the glass £7.50. House white/red £13.50.
When is it open?	Monday to Wednesday 6pm-11pm. Thursday to Sunday Noon-11pm.
Get in touch	268 Woodstock Road Oxford OX2 7NW ✆ 01865 311936 www.thelemontreeoxford.co.uk

LOCATION SCOUT: KATE ROUSE

Cibo! Oxford

Gossip & Secrets

The food	Modern Italian. Great choice of starters, pasta (seafood, meat and vegetarian), risottos, fish and meat dishes.
The drink	Frascati, Soave and Pinot Grigio of course, but also some hearty reds, plus aperitifs and cocktails.
Why is it so good?	Freshly prepared, tasty Italian food without a chewy pizza in sight. Friendly staff. Relaxed atmosphere.
Why is it not so good?	A little characterless towards the back of the restaurant, where you miss the buzz.
To die for	Whole sea bass cooked on the charcoal grill (£13.95).
Occasions	Couples, groups of friends or families. The private dining room also seats 16.
When to go	Lunchtime for a shopper's break or business lunch, or mellow evenings.
Atmosphere	Contemporary Italian, with comfortable leather sofas in the bar area for drinks/coffee and great use of mirrors and lighting in the dining area.
In the know	Collapse in one of the armchairs for a pre-Saturday lunch drink and catch up on the newspapers.

Essentials

How big?	Deceptively sizeable – but popular, so try to book in advance.
Where is it?	In the "restaurant souk" of South Parade in Summertown, between Banbury and Woodstock Roads.
How much?	Starters – £2.75 to £6.95 Mains – £5.95 to £16.95 House wine from £12.50. Good selection in the £15-£22 range.
When is it open?	Monday to Saturday 12pm-2.30pm for lunch, 6pm to 10.30 for dinner. Drinks or coffee served from 10.30am-3.30pm and 6.30pm-11.00pm.
Get in touch	4 South Parade Summertown Oxford OX2 7JL ✆ 01865 292321 www.ilovecibo.co.uk

LOCATION SCOUT: PAUL ROUSE

Summertown Wine Café Oxford

Gossip & Secrets

The food	Just enough to soak up, and complement, the wine. Great fresh platters of cheeses, cold meats, pate and olives. Daily specials.
The drink	Wine tasting is the name of the game. This is not a snooty wine shop: the staff are down to earth, and allow you to work out flavours and tastes so that you can order a wine you enjoy.
Why is it so good?	The wine is classed as boutique wine: from small growers and bought in small quantities. No supermarket giants here. The list changes monthly and includes favourites and superstars. You can buy the wine to take home, or drink it here.
To die for	Wine that would normally cost you £40-plus in a restaurant is sold here at retail price plus £2.50 corkage.
When to go	Busy in the evenings with drinkers, so daytimes for some serous wine tasting.
Atmosphere	Laid back (the owner is Australian) but quietly fashionable.
In the know	Join The Nude Bottle Society. A chance to create wine art and get lots of invites to selection panels and special evenings.

Essentials

How big?	Smallish at the front. Spacious conservatory area at the rear.
How much?	Food platters from £5, house wine £7.50 to take home, or £10 to drink in the café. Wide wine choice from £12.50
When is it open?	8am – 11pm
Get in touch	38 South Parade Summertown Oxford OX2 7JN ✆ 01865 558800

LOCATION SCOUT: KATE ROUSE

Bar Meze Oxford

Gossip & Secrets

The food	Turkish. Incredible choice of hot and cold meze, ideal to share. Try borek (filo pastry filled with feta cheese) or incik (slow roasted lamb on the bone). Good selection for vegetarians.
The drink	Good quality New World wines from £13. Try the Turkish Efes beer or the Turkish Villa Dolluca wine.
Why is it so good?	Friendly, helpful staff who really want you to enjoy your Turkish experience. Extensive menu, delicious food, generous portions.
Why is it not so good?	Can get really busy with large parties.
To die for	Baklava served with Cornish clotted cream: crumbly layers of filo pastry crammed full of cashew nuts and sweet scented syrup with a big dollop of clotted cream ...orgasmic!
When to go	If you like it lively, go on Friday or Saturday nights, but best to book early. Lunchtimes are usually quieter, but can get busy with shoppers and business lunches.
Atmosphere	Busy, lively, fun — everyone, including the staff, seem to be enjoying themselves. Very Turkish feel: copper tables, big comfy leather sofas, and mainly circular tables, ideal for dining with friends.
In the know	If you've not tried Turkish food before or just want to take advantage of their special lunchtime offer: two meze dishes, glass of wine or soft drink and coffee costs £6.00.

Essentials

How big?	Comfortably seat 85 people.
Where is it?	On the main road into Headington.
How much?	Average starter meze — £8.00 for three dishes, £14 for six dishes, £18 for nine dishes. Main meze — £12-£14. Desserts — £5.00.
When is it open?	Lunch and evenings seven days a week.
Get in touch	146 London Road Headington Oxford OX3 9ED
	✆ 01865 761106
	www.bar-meze.co.uk

LOCATION SCOUT: ALISON PETRASH

Isis Tavern Oxford

Gossip & Secrets

The food	Good, wholesome, inexpensive home-cooked pub grub.
The drink	Normal pub selection plus three real ales – Speckled Hen, IPA and Abbot Ale.
Why is it so good?	Perfect location right by the river. Big enclosed garden is great for children.
Why is it not so good?	Gets very busy in fine weather so sometimes there is a wait for food.
To die for	If you have been on a long walk by the Thames, it is great to know that you can sit and relax over a delicious pint of ale. Unpretentious surroundings and fabulous location.
When to go	Best time is when the weather is good so you can sit outside on one of the picnic benches. Sunday lunch is good and so are the evenings.
Atmosphere	Very casual. Pub has a river theme with a boat hanging from the rafters. Two log fires are kept going in the winter. Bar billiards table.
In the know	The skittle alley (reputably haunted) can be booked for groups of 8 or more.

Essentials

Run by	Andy and Veronica Jardine.
How big?	About 50 tables outside. Inside seating is limited.
Where is it?	On the towpath at Iffley Lock. You can only reach it on foot.
How much?	Main courses from £6.50. Desserts £4.00. Sunday lunch: Roast selection from £5.95.
When is it open?	Pub hours. Food served until 9pm every day.
Get in touch	The Towing Path Oxford OX4 4EL ✆ 01865 247006

LOCATION SCOUT: MICHAEL COCKMAN

Talk of the **town**

Close to the centre of Oxford but in a quiet village setting, The Fishes combines the best of both worlds.

The Fishes
North Hinksey Village
Oxford
OX2 0NA
☏ 01865 249796
www.fishesoxford.co.uk

village setting belies the fact it is minutes from the centre of Oxford.

This is a pub with great food — it is not a restaurant masquerading as a pub. Owned by the small independent group Peach Pubs, they appear have added yet another great place to their list of very successful establishments throughout Oxfordshire, Warwickshire and Bedfordshire..

THE GREAT OUTDOORS

Food-wise, The Fishes has hit the spot, becoming one of the most talked-about places in Oxford. A combination of high quality, ethically-sourced food, plus the flair and passion of the staff, has created a menu that deserves several visits.

Firstly of course, no Peach Pub would be a Peach if it didn't have the deli board. Choose from cold cuts, cheese, fish, or a selection that includes apples, grapes, melon, pickles, houmous, pickled onions, olives and sun-dried tomatoes: a meal in itself.

From the main menu, there are weekly-changing risotto and sausage specials, plus Caesar salad, steak & chips (aged 35 days — delicious), or one of the house specialities, a rack of lamb served on a board with baby roast potatoes, gravy and béarnaise: £30 for two and enough to finish you off for the day. A seasonally-changing menu may include lobster, crab and avocado salad, as well as spinach and mushroom pancakes, or a rare roast beef salad with horseradish crème fraiche.

Outdoors, the pub has a great decking terrace, with gas heaters to keep you warm when the weather cools. The gardens run down to the river, and on a good day, my vote has to be to grab a picnic blanket and hamper from the bar. All deli boards can be hamper-packed, alongside favourites like a BLT, Scotch beef burgers, roast free-range chicken or cold chicken & ham pie. Crack open the bubbly, ring your friends, and chill.

Where have all the good pubs gone? A cry heard from many a saddened heart when they see their favourite local taken over by new owners and turned into some fancy 'gastro pub', with expensive wines and dining-only areas. The alternative — those that have had nothing done to them as the purists try to hang on the 'romance' of smoke-filled bars and old men playing dominoes — has equally limited appeal. How about a place that should be what a pub was meant to be? A place to wind down, to drink, eat, meet and relax.

I think I have found such a place. Opening its newly refurbished doors in summer 2005, The Fishes has all the cool, modern and even slightly trendy look of the 'gastro pub' But look closer and you will also find an old-fashioned snug, a bar with stools to prop on and chat at your leisure, and the option to eat when you want and, most importantly, where you want. What's more, its

DECiSiON TiME

Good pubs normally mean good staff, and The Fishes has got it just right: friendly, welcoming, genuinely pleased to see you, and keen to help. I chatted with a few and began to understand why. The manager Natalie is down-to-earth, bubbly, and is obviously liked and respected by her staff. She trusts them to make decisions: if something is not quite right with your meal, your waiter or waitress will sort it out. None of this ridiculous 'I will have to go and talk to my manager' routine, which personally drives me mad.

The staff are a mix of British and Antipodeans. As gap year travellers, the latter are enjoying the experience, and it shows. The company, I found out, has a training creed that aims to "undersell and over-deliver". So no cheesy lines to convince you to have the larger salad, extra dessert or an expensive wine. They aim to offer you what you want, and as a result, you want to go back, because you enjoyed the experience so much. This is a relaxed, informal, fun place that also happens to serve exceptionally good food. But a word of warning: phone first and book. ∫∫

REVIEW: Kate Rouse

ESSENTiALS

Run by Hamish Stoddart and Natalie Langman.
How big 60 inside and another 40 on the terrace, plus an extensive garden.
How much Average starter £4-£6
Average main £8-£13
Average dessert £4.50
Children Very welcome
Get in touch North Hinksey Village
Oxford
OX2 0NA
✆ 01865 249796
www.fishesoxford.co.uk
fishes@peachpubs.com

GOSSiP & SECRETS

The food Modern classics. You must try the picnic hampers.
The drink Wide selection of wines and spirits.
To die for Deli boards – over 20 different choices to build your own. Or the rack of Cornish Lamb on a board for two.
When to go Sunny days – huge garden with picnic benches, rugs and hampers. Winter days will be cosy and snug.
Atmosphere Informal but efficient.
The knowledge There is an excellent all-day menu for flexible eating.
Don't just take our word for it Everyone's talking about it!

LOCATION SCOUT Suzanne Lockhart

LOCATION PARTNER

An inspector **calls**

Morse is just one of many famous names associated with Oxford's grandest hotel.

Situated opposite the Ashmolean Museum and built in 1864, the Randolph is one of Oxford's most famous landmarks. It exudes gothic elegance, and if those walls could only talk! Host to such luminaries as Bill Clinton and Monica Lewinsky (apparently not at the same time), the Randolph has a timeless charm. Enjoying afternoon tea in the beautiful drawing room, it is easy to imagine Miss Marple sitting opposite in a high-backed chair.

In reality, the Randolph owes its current television fame to another detective, Inspector Morse. The author of the books, Colin Dexter, is a regular, and the hotel features in many of the books and TV programmes, so much so that the cocktail bar is now known as The Morse Bar, and the walls are adorned with pictures of John Thaw and company. The hotel is still a favourite with the crew, and they have been back again recently for the sequel, which sees Kevin Whately promoted to Inspector Lewis.

SPA TREATMENT

With soaring arches and a stunning lobby, the hotel is romantic, yet doesn't overwhelm you. The 151 rooms, located in either the original building or the brand-new wing, sit alongside a modern spa built into the cellars, offering a tranquil escape from the buzz of the city, with aroma steam rooms, a bio sauna and an ice fountain. Treatments are by Decleor and hotel guests are given priority on treatments.

Bedrooms are spacious, and the suites are heavenly. The new rooms are calming and have lovely walk-in showers with separate baths. The dilemma is: a new room for the bathroom, or an older room for the sense of drama?

The Randolph offers all the trimmings you would expect from such an Oxford institution, and its restaurant is wonderful, whilst the Morse Bar is a favourite place for pre-theatre drinks, as the Playhouse is next door. It doesn't take much detective work to discover that this is one of the best places in Oxford for people-watching. ∫∫.

CLASSIC
LOCATIONS
FAVOURITE

ESSENTIALS

Run by Stephanie Hocking, General Manager. Part of Macdonald Hotels.

How big 151 rooms. Restaurant can seat 90. Private dining and conference facilities can accommodate up to 220 for a dinner & dance.

How much Accommodation: Check the website for room rates as different tariffs run at different times.

Restaurant: Table d'hote – £19 (2 courses), £24 (3 courses).

Sunday lunch: £15.50 (2 courses),

£20 (3 courses).

A la carte: average starter – £6.50

average main – £17-£22

average dessert – £6.50

Children Easily accommodated.

Get in touch The Randolph Hotel

Beaumont Street

Oxford OX1 2LN

✆ 0870 400 8200

www.randolph-hotel.com

GOSSIP & SECRETS

The food For any special occasion, from romance to business, you know you will get classic food with a contemporary twist.

The drink Great bar with lots of atmosphere. Champagne cocktails and a great wine list rub shoulders with good beer. Morse knew a thing or two.

To die for Afternoon tea in the drawing room.

When to go Pre-theatre supper and drinks. Sunday lunch and romantic getaways that require access to lots of things to do: the Randolph is in the heart of the city centre.

Atmosphere Agatha Christie meets Inspector Morse.

The knowledge The bar is frequented by many famous residents of Oxford, and lots of the film crews that come to Oxford stay at the Randolph. Good place for a bit of celebrity spotting!

Don't just take our word for it
AA 4-star.

LOCATION
PARTNER

Heart **of the matter**

Luxury accommodation at an affordable price – the Eastgate makes the most of its central location.

One of the reasons for writing this book was to uncover the secrets of a location, places that you might not necessarily find by looking at other guide books or searching the web.

The Eastgate Townhouse is one of those places.

Small but perfectly formed, it is almost unrivalled in location, in the heart of the city, with extremely distinguished college neighbours. Opposite Ruskin, next to Merton and overlooking Magdalen, this recently-renovated elegant townhouse has been part of Oxford's history since the 17th century, with the current building dating from around 1900.

Sixty-three bedrooms nestle into the bottom end of the High Street, with immediate access to the shops, restaurants and bars of one of Oxford's most famous thoroughfares. Offering, in essence, a luxury bed and breakfast service for a remarkable rate, this hotel is an ideal base for anyone looking for accessibility without the fuss of a full-service hotel. Frequented by visiting academics, international tourists and business visitors wishing for a more informal stay in Oxford, the Eastgate Townhouse offers very friendly service from multicultural staff, one of the best breakfasts in the city, and that most treasured of amenities in Oxford — a car park!

FiRiNG THE iMAGiNATiON

Merton's Bar at the front of the hotel, with access directly from the High Street and open to non-residents, is a popular watering hole for students, academics, locals and visitors, and has a rich history all to itself: Oxford don and writer CS Lewis even proposed to Joy Gresham here. The hotel entrance itself is on Merton Street, a popular film location, as one of the only remaining cobbled streets in the city. With very little sign of modern times, at night its atmosphere takes hold of your imagination: listen carefully, and you can almost hear the sound of carriages and horses' hooves pass by! ∬

CLASSIC
LOCATiONS

HIDDEN SECRETS

41

ESSENTiALS

Run by Frank Harvey, General Manager.

How big 63 bedrooms. Some rooms look over the colleges. Restaurant seats 43 and is only open for breakfast.

How much Sunday to Thursday from £89 per room. Friday & Saturday from £109 per room.

Children Very welcome.

Get in touch 73 The High Street
Oxford OX1 4BE
☎ 0870 400 8201
www.macdonaldhotels.co.uk

GOSSiP & SECRETS

The food Breakfast only, but step out of the front door of the hotel and you are slap bang in the middle of the city for a wide choice.

The drink Tea and coffee facilities in the room. Merton's Bar is open until 2am. Whilst part of the hotel, it actually has its own entrance, and the noise does not impinge on the hotel at all.

To die for Location, location, location.

When to go Summer for views over the city with golden honey hues, winter for Christmas shopping without the the hassle! Also a great place to enjoy the May Day celebrations at nearby Magdalen Bridge.

Atmosphere Elegant, friendly, not stuffy and very relaxed.

The knowledge Great boardroom overlooking Ruskin College if you need to combine business with pleasure. The car park is only £12.50 per 24 hours, is fully secure, and offers valet parking.

Don't just take our word for it AA 3-star.

LOCATiON
PARTNER

Old Parsonage Hotel Oxford

Gossip & Secrets

The food	In good weather, sit on the terrace and enjoy lobster grills and champagne. In winter, savour the restaurant. Not surprisingly, this sister property to Gee's serves a similar style of modern English food, with fresh fish flown in daily from Jersey.
The drink	This is sundowner territory. The ideal place to have a glass or two after shopping, before dinner, pre- or post-theatre, or simply a rather stylish place to meet friends.
Why is it so good?	Situated in a 17th century parsonage, the bar and terrace of this small yet perfectly positioned hotel is one of Oxford's best kept secrets.
	Small, charmingly English, yet with a recent re-furbishment that puts it into a modern, almost boutique hotel bracket. Great art on the walls as the owner (Jeremy Mogford) has a passion for collecting graduation art from talented individuals.
Why is it not so good?	The old and not so great of Oxford still hang on to the place for afternoon tea, which pushes the average age up quite a bit! And the traffic noise can be a pain at times.
To die for	Jazz on a Friday evening in the summer on the terrace.
Atmosphere	Country house in the middle of a city.
In the know	Private dining in the Pike room for 12. A superb herb garden on the roof for quiet drinks.

Essentials

How big?	30 bedrooms. 60 covers in main bar/restaurant. 44 on the terrace in good weather.
Where is it?	In St Giles, next to the church. Blink and you'll miss the walled entrance. A handful of parking spaces if you are lucky.
How much?	Average starter £8-£10; mains £17-£20; desserts £6. House wine £10.50. Rooms from £155 for a double.
Get in touch	1 Banbury Road Oxford OX2 6NN ✆ 01865 310210 www.oldparsonage-hotel.co.uk

LOCATION SCOUT: KATE ROUSE

THE ST. GILES AREA IS ADJACENT TO THE OLD PARSONAGE ▶

Covered Market Oxford

Gossip & Secrets

What is it?	Built in the 1770's as Oxford's main food market. Now also includes a variety of fashions, luxury goods and specialist shops, plus cafes galore.
Where is it?	Between the High Street, Market Street and Cornmarket Street.
What makes it special?	The history. The character. The atmosphere. The range of goods. And the smells of fresh food!
Best for food:	Oxford Cheese Company – home of the famous Oxford Blue plus a host of fabulous British and international cheeses.
	Fasta Pasta – homemade sandwiches and deli.
	David John – mouthwatering pork pies.
	Palm's Delicatessen – jams and preserves, plus perfect gift hampers.
	Fruitsticks – fresh fruit smoothies.
	M. Feller – organic butchers. Like they used to be.
	Aunty May's Pasty Co – delicious fresh-baked Cornish pasties. Padstow eat your heart out.
	Ben's Cookies – heavenly smells.
Best for fashion:	Two Foot Nothing – unusual children's clothes.
	The Hat Box – weddings a speciality.
	Oxford Boot Store – for urban cowboys.
Best for interiors:	Red Opia – distinctive furniture and fabrics from the Far East.
Best for gifts:	Covered Arts – limited edition prints and a framing service. Look out for Wendy Skinner's superb paintings of modern Oxford.
	The Garden – flowers for all occasions and great pots.
When is it open?	Monday to Saturday, 8.30am to 5.30pm

LOCATION SCOUT: PAUL ROUSE

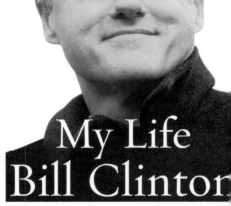

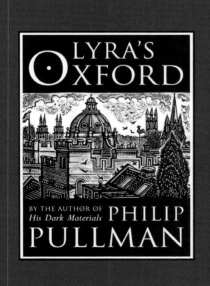

Blackwell's Bookshop Oxford

Gossip & Secrets

The history	An Oxford institution since 1879.
Size	Enormous! Spreads over three floors, but that hardly does justice to the labyrinth of rooms, sections and tucked-away corners. A tourist attraction in its own right.
Where is it?	Main shop on Broad Street, opposite the Sheldonian. Across the road you will find the specialist Art + Poster shop and the Music shop.
	Also branches at Oxford Brookes University in Headington and a medical bookshop at The John Radcliffe Hospital.
What makes it special?	Size, scale, scope. Somewhere to lose yourself for hours, or find exactly what you are looking for. If Blackwell's don't stock it — or can't order it for you — it probably doesn't exist.
What's there?	A complete cross-section of fiction and non-fiction, specialist departments, academic and text books, a second-hand section, and a Rare Books shop selling first and limited editions.
Best bit?	The travel section. Every travel book you could wish for on Oxford (including this one) and a wide variety of UK and international travel books, which then dovetails into associated books such as the language, history, politics and society of every country.
Refreshment	The busy coffee shop for a cappuccino and Danish, or pop next door (actually right in the middle!) to the White Horse for a pint.
Not just a bookshop	Blackwell's is one of the major sponsors of the annual Oxford Literary Festival, a week-long event of readings, talks, book signings and literature-related activities, which draws writers as diverse as Melvyn Bragg, Jung Chang, Joanne Harris, Will Self and PD James.
Other activities	Blackwell's organises regular reading groups, and offers a series of guided walking tours, covering historic and literary Oxford.

Essentials

When is it open?	Monday to Saturday 9am-6pm, Sunday 11am-7pm
Get in touch	48-51 Broad Street Oxford OX1 3BQ ✆ 01865 792792 www.blackwell.co.uk

LOCATION SCOUT: PAUL ROUSE

◀ BLACKWELL'S BOOKSHOP, ONE OF OXFORD'S INSTITUTIONS

High Street Oxford

Gossip & Secrets

What is it?	Oxford's most famous thoroughfare. Lined with Tudor, Georgian and Victorian buildings, not to mention several splendid university colleges. Known to locals as The High.
Where is it?	Runs from the corner of St Aldates and Cornmarket Street down to Magdalen Bridge
What makes it special?	A mix of small specialist shops, pubs, cafes and restaurants. Mercifully free of too many "high street" brand names — and the ones that are there are generally of the upmarket variety.
Fashion	Narda Artwear, Agnis B, Glasshouse, Kaliko, Hobbs, Phase Eight, Jigsaw, Karen Millen, Coast, Whistles, White Stuff, Sahara.
Specialists	Pens Plus — stylish writing implements.
	Hoyles — games and puzzles.
	Antiques On High.
	Sanders — old maps and prints.
	Whittard — premium teas and coffees.
	Molton Brown — posh toiletries.
	Neal's Yard — remedies and therapies.
	Frederick Tranter — old-fashioned tobacconist.
University connections	University of Oxford shop — officially approved branded products.
	Oxford University Press — text and academic books.
	Ede & Ravenscroft — academic gowns.
Food and drink	The Grand Café, Quod, Cafe Zouk, Queen's Lane Coffee House, The Rose, All Bar One.
Nooks and crannies	Fascinating side streets, including Turl Street, Alfred Street, Blue Boar Street, Bear Lane, King Edward Street, Magpie Lane, Catte Street, Oriel Street, Queen's Lane.

North Parade Avenue Oxford

Gossip & Secrets

What is it?	One small street, but a tiny corner of Bohemia amongst the otherwise grand houses of suburban Oxford.
Where is it?	Off Banbury Road – coming out of town, turn left just past Gee's restaurant.
What makes it special?	An eclectic mix of small specialist shops, pubs, cafes and restaurants. Bright colours and bunting mark it out amongst the greys and browns of Victorian property.
Food and drink:	Chez Gaston for crepes.
	Luna Caprese for old-fashioned Italian.
	Bon Appetit for deli delights.
	Le Parisien for French patisseries.
	Bagicha for a taste of India.
	On The Hoof for sandwiches.
	Plus two pubs – the Rose & Crown and the Gardener's Arms.
Art:	The Verandah and Taurus galleries, for original artwork and limited edition prints.
Gifts:	Pula for ethnic gifts and artwork.
Gardens:	Home Garden for specialist products, prints, accessories and landscaping services.
Style:	Pophams, hairdresser to the yummie mummy brigade.
The shop(s) around the corner:	Liscious for unusual interiors and Oxford Violins for … you guessed.
When is it open?	Times vary, but the shops tend to open normal hours, Monday to Saturday. The pubs and restaurants stay open in the evenings.

LOCATION SCOUT: PAUL ROUSE

Mister Wolf

Colin McNaughton

Sarah Wiseman Gallery Oxford

Essentials

Style	Sophisticated and friendly art gallery with a knowledgeable curator/owner and a very interesting range of artists.
Size	A spacious room on two levels.
Cost	A variety of artists to suit everyone, from serious collectors to those wanting a one-off piece for a special place.
What makes it special?	Sarah has a personal touch and gets to know what lies behind the work. This is reflected in the collections and pieces she chooses. A wide range of artists and themed exhibitions are on show throughout the year.
Where is it?	Summertown, one of north Oxford's upmarket suburbs. Close to some good restaurants and bars, so you can always celebrate your art purchases.
Get in touch	40-41 South Parade Summertown Oxford OX2 7JL. ✆ 01865 515123 www.wisegal.com

LOCATION SCOUT: AMANDA WYATT

Vanilla Oxford

Essentials

Style	Relaxed yet professional with lovely combination of colourful clothes and accessories.
Size	Small but perfectly formed.
Cost	Value-for-money designer labels and smaller items ideal for gifts.
Exclusive stockists of:	Diane Von Fursenberg, Missoni Sport, Transit, Masons, John Smedley, Antik Batik, Day, Lilith, John Laing, Joie, Ann-Louise Roswald, Diptyque, Sportmeax and lots more.
In the know	Vanilla Shoes, next door, has a wonderful selection in all colours and styles.
Get in touch	13 South Parade Summertown Oxford OX2 7JN. ⌀ 01865 552155 www.vanillalife.com

LOCATION SCOUT: AMANDA WYATT

Marmalade Oxford

Essentials

What is it?	Shop? Eat? Visit? All three. Wears its heart on its sleeve supporting local artists, sells furniture, and provides home-cooked organic food.
Where is it?	A hidden treasure, tucked away in several light rooms behind the Jam Factory but only two minutes walk from the train station. Frequently changing exhibitions of fine art, photography and prints.
Cost	Free admission.
What makes it special?	Talented local artists, comfy sofas, a relaxed atmosphere and an old piano — a really welcoming place.
Best bit?	Not everyone knows it's there yet, so great place to take people for the first time.
Food options	Recipes from around the world. Inexpensive and good quality.
Got to see/do	Take a chance on who will be exhibiting in the gallery, and then try the marmalade ice cream in the cafe.
Get in touch	The Old Jam Factory 27 Park End Street Oxford OX1 1HU ✆ 01865 244613 www.marmaladegallery.net

LOCATION SCOUT: JANINE CHARLES

Arcadia Oxford

Essentials

Style	Gift, card and second hand book shop with a romantic, old-fashioned feel. Great music.
Size	Small: three adjoining rooms on one level.
Cost	Something for every budget. Look through the half price card box for some great bargains.
Exclusive stockists of:	The only place to source old copies of Vogue, Playboy and other magazines in Oxford. A great selection of old postcards.
Where is it?	Tucked away off Cornmarket Street.
Get in touch	4 St Michaels Street Oxford OX1 2DU ✆ 01865 241757

LOCATION SCOUT: KATHRYN SMITH

LB's Oxford

Gossip & Secrets

The food	If you've never been to Beirut – then this is as close as you will get. Fantastic mezze dishes which you can eat in the cafe or take away to create a meal at home. Everything is made from the best possible ingredients, with lots of Lebanese specialities on offer. Great shawarmas, the Lebanese sandwich: Arabic flatbread filled with chicken or lamb with pickles, tomatoes, parsley and hommos.
The drink	Freshly squeezed orange juice and standard soft drinks. No alcohol.
Why is it so good?	I often buy a whole range of dishes for a last minute dinner party.
Why is it not so good?	Should be open later than 7pm!
To die for	The sweet counter. Traditional baklawa, maamoul and scrummy raha (Turkish delight).
Atmosphere	Basic cafe: clean and simply furnished.
In the know	Daily lunch specials are remarkable value, and vegetarians are very well catered for with Lebanese food.

Essentials

How big?	A handful of people can eat inside. This is a takeaway/deli/café.
Where is it?	Summertown. Parking in the large municipal car park is normally the best option; the free parking in front of LB's is normally full.
How much?	A takeaway meal for four people: average £16-20. Shawarma – £2.
When is it open?	Monday to Friday 9am-7pm. Saturday 9-6pm. Sunday 10-4pm.
Get in touch	235 Banbury Road Oxford OX2 7HN
	✆ 01865 311660
	www.lbs.oxfordpages.co.uk

LOCATION SCOUT: KATE ROUSE

A city of books Oxford

Gossip & Secrets

The history	As one of the world's great university cities, a centre of publishing, and the home of the Sunday Times Oxford Literary Festival, it comes as no surprise that Oxford has scores of great bookshops.
The big players	Blackwell's — see separate feature.
	Borders — part of the national chain. Prime position on Magdalen Street. Vast selection on a wide range of subjects. Superb magazine section. Also sells music CDs. Café and bookshop open Monday to Saturday 9am-11pm and Sunday 11am-5pm.
	Waterstone's — the other big national. Corner of Broad Street and Cornmarket Street. Complete A-Z selection. Numerous book signings. Also sells calendars and postcards. Excellent Books Quarterly magazine (a group publication) for reviews and recommendations. Costa Coffee shop and bookstore open 9am-7pm Monday to Saturday (8pm Thursdays) and Sunday 11am-5pm.
The specialists	Dozens of smaller shops selling rare, secondhand and books on specific topics. Favourites include St. Philip's Bookshop and Reservoir Bookshop, both on St. Aldates, the Jericho Bookshop on Walton Street, and Waterfield's on the High Street. As the headquarters of Oxfam, Oxford also has two great Oxfam bookshops, on Turl Street and St. Giles.
The publishers	Major companies such as Oxford University Press, Heinemann and Elsevier, plus numerous publishers of academic, educational, scientific and medical books.
Home grown success	Small Oxford publisher David Fickling Books hit the big time with local authors Philip Pullman and Mark Haddon.
Get in touch	Oxford Literary Festival www.sundaytimes-oxfordliteraryfestival.co.uk

LOCATION SCOUT: PAUL ROUSE

Essentials

What is it?	Bookshop, cafe-bar and members' club, housed in a historic building just off Broad Street.
Style	Intellectual, but trying not to be too snooty. QI stands for Quite Interesting – the pre-requisite of being a customer or member.
Quite Interesting?	Co-owned by TV producer John Lloyd, of Blackadder and Not The Nine O'Clock News fame. His latest venture is, of course, the quiz show QI hosted by Stephen Fry.
Size	Small specialist bookshop downstairs – eclectic mix of religion, philosophy, sociology and other books you might not find elsewhere. Cafe-bar also on the ground floor. Private rooms available upstairs.
What is so good about it?	Quiet haven amid the central Oxford bustle. Subterranean vodka bar.
What is not so good about it?	Publicity-shy, despite its origins. Easily missed.
Food options	Light snacks from £4-£7, main courses from £7-£14.
When is it open?	Monday to Saturday 10am-11pm.
Get in touch	16 Turl Street Oxford OX1 3DH Ø 01865 261501 www.qi.com

LOCATION SCOUT: PAUL ROUSE

THE QI BOOKSHOP

Heaven **sent**

A stylish day spa in the centre of Oxford, Heavenly Bodies delivers exactly that.

Well thank goodness for Tracey Dunlop. Tracey is the owner and creator of Heavenly Bodies. Three years ago she was earning a six-digit salary, when for some bizarre reason, having seen that 23 Beaumont Street was empty, she decided to quit the IT industry and set up her dream spa. Over £500K later and she has a thriving, sexy, grown-up spa, equally open and comfortable to men and women, and offering the highest standard of treatment from really talented staff using great products. She has male and female staff and from the moment you walk into this fabulous Georgian House, you know you are in for a special treat.

GLORIOUS MUD

I felt as though I had walked into a private club when I arrived for three and a half hours of 'me' time. Warm burgundies and rich reds mix with gold to create a welcoming ambiance, and stunning artwork hangs on the walls as a result of a deal with a local art gallery. (If you like what you see, prepare to pay around £1K for each picture, they are really fabulous!). I was escorted to the relaxation room where I waited for my therapist to come and find me.

My first treatment was the Rasul steam, and I was rather pleased I had dragged my husband along. We were led into a small room that reminded me of the hammans we visited in Jordan. Presented with a plate of medicinal charka muds, we locked the door and merrily indulged in rubbing mud into each other. (Suggestion! If you come with a friend rather than a partner, make sure you bring a swimming costume or know each very well: naked romps with mud definitely do conjure up some, shall we say, interesting thoughts!). With different muds for each part of the body, we started at the top and … worked our way down.

We were then plunged into darkness, with a twinkle-star roof supplying the only light for the next 45 minutes. A hiss signalled the start of the steam, and as we relaxed, we sweated and giggled through

Stress is apparently the 21st century's must-have problem. Everyone you speak to is suffering from stress. Companies have stress management courses, people are addicted to quizzes that identify 'how stressed' you are, and doctors' surgeries are full of patients with stress-related illness. But I have found a cure. Spend some time at Heavenly Bodies Day Spa in the centre of Oxford and your stress will be long-forgotten.

Mention a spa to most people and the instant image is of lots of twittering women. Pink and girlie are the words that spring to mind, and the only men in sight are the ones very much in touch with their feminine side! The image is of sterile treatment rooms, over-manicured perfect beauticians who make you feel even more insecure than the perfectly made-up cosmetic counter staff, and not an ounce of cellulite in sight.

the dark at each other. When the lights come back on, a tropical shower falls from the roof to rinse off the mud. The result: clean soft skin that felt tremendous and ready for stage two, a deep tissue massage and a facial to follow that left both of us shiny, relaxed and not a trace of stress in sight.

THE GREAT ESCAPE

Heavenly Bodies works works with brands that include Elemis. You can book individual treatments or groups, from hen days to gossip days. Tracey and her team are completely flexible to ensure that your time spent at Heavenly Bodies is as relaxing and fulfilling as possible.

The spa has been open for two years and is starting to build an enviable reputation for massage therapy. Standard treatments such as deep relaxation and aromatherapy are available, but sports injury and chronic pain treatment can also be booked. My deep tissue massage, whilst perhaps not the most heavenly experience (in fact it hurt like hell!) has cleared headaches and left me feeling far less knotted and tight than almost anything else I have experienced.

This is a spa to relax in and escape; grown-up, chic and creating new standards in the day spa market. Go on. Spoil yourself and leave behind 21st century stress! ʃʃ

SECRET ESSENTIALS

Run by Tracey Dunlop.
How big 9 treatment rooms.
How much Facial £30-£70
Massage £30-£70
Manicure & Pedicure £20-£35
Rasul Steam for two £60
Packages from £45
Children No – this is a kid-free, stress-free zone!
Get in touch 23 Beaumont Street
Oxford OX1 2NP
✆ 01865 723577
info@heavenlybodiesdayspa.com
www.heavenlybodiesdayspa.com

GOSSIP & SECRETS

The food Lunch is available but needs to be pre-ordered as they have no actual restaurant on site, but will cater for your requirements in the relaxation room.
The drink Champagne or whatever you fancy can be ordered for special occasions. Tea, coffee and water is freely available.
To die for Rasul for two: very sexy, very relaxing, and very different.
When to go Anytime. They are open 7 days a week. Weekends can get busy, so book in advance
Atmosphere Sexy, grown up, great for friends or couples as men feel very comfortable in this non-pink, non-fluffy environment (my other half loves it here!)
The knowledge Watch the web site. Tracey has big expansion plans and wants to take the Heavenly Bodies concept to other city centres in equally spectacular style. Quote Classic Locations when booking more than £50 worth of treatments and get a free Rasul for two worth £60.
Don't just take our word for it Voted one of the top 16 spas on earth by Elle magazine. One of Harpers & Queen's top 100 spas in the world. Voted as one of the top 10 Mother's Day treats by the Daily Express.

LOCATION SCOUT Kate Rouse

LOCATION PARTNER

Alma Mater Famous students

The history	With its origins in the 12th century, Oxford is the oldest English-speaking university in the world. It has produced thousands of distinguished graduates in all walks of life.
The students	Kings, politicians, archbishops, scientists, artists, writers and performers, including 25 British Prime Ministers, 46 Nobel prize winners, and even three saints.
Prime Ministers	Peel, Gladstone and Asquith, plus eight from the post-war period: Attlee, Eden, Macmillan, Douglas-Home, Wilson, Heath, Thatcher and Blair.
Politicians	Thomas More, Indira Gandhi, Tony Benn, Shirley Williams, Bob Hawke, Bill Clinton, Barbara Castle and Boris Johnson.
Religious leaders	Cardinal Wolsey, John Wesley, Cardinal Basil Hume, Robert Runcie and Rowan Williams.
Scholars and philosophers	Roger Bacon, Erasmus and Thomas Hobbes.
Explorers	Sir Walter Raleigh and Sir Richard Burton.
Art and science	Christopher Wren, Edmund Halley, William Morris, Edwin Hubble and Stephen Hawking.
Writers and poets	John Donne, Jonathan Swift, Matthew Arnold, Lewis Carroll, Gerard Manley Hopkins, Oscar Wilde, John Buchan, JRR Tolkien, TS Eliot, Aldous Huxley, CS Lewis, Robert Graves, Graham Greene, Evelyn Waugh, Cecil Day Lewis, WH Auden, Kingsley Amis, Iris Murdoch, Philip Larkin, Alan Bennett, Julian Barnes, William Boyd, Monica Ali and Mark Haddon.
Film and theatre	Lindsay Anderson, Ken Loach, Dudley Moore, Maria Aitken, Rowan Atkinson, Hugh Grant, Imogen Stubbs, Emilia Fox and Rosamund Pike.
TV and media	David Dimbleby, Michael Palin, Rick Stein, Nigella Lawson, Oz Clark, Ian Hislop, Natasha Kaplinsky, Rageh Omaar and Fiona Bruce.
Badge of honour	You never need to ask anybody if they studied at Oxford. They will always tell you.
Bluffer's guide	Going to Oxford Brookes University is not quite the same thing as "going to Oxford." Nor was Jeffery Archer's stint at the Oxford Department of Education.

◄ FAMOUS FACES (CLOCKWISE FROM TOP LEFT): ROWAN ATKINSON; NATASHA KAPLINSKY; OZ CLARK; BILL CLINTON; RAGEH OMAAR; NIGELLA LAWSON; HUGH GRANT; MICHAEL PALIN; IAN HISLOP

On Location: Oxford in the movies

The backdrop:	With its rich history and academic heritage, Oxford has been a popular setting for a host of films, mainly set in the past.
The famous ones:	Another Country (1984) starring Rupert Everett and Colin Firth
	Howard's End (1992) starring Anthony Hopkins and Emma Thompson
	Shadowlands (1993) starring Anthony Hopkins and Debra Winger
	The Madness of King George (1994) starring Nigel Hawthorne and Rupert Everett
	Wilde (1997) starring Stephen Fry and Jude Law
	Quills (2000) staring Kate Winslet and Geoffrey Rush
	Iris (2001) starring Judi Dench and Jim Broadbent
	… and not forgetting Harry Potter (see overleaf)
The not-so famous ones:	American Friends (1991) starring Michael Palin as his own grandfather
	The Saint (1997) starring Val Kilmer as Simon Templar
	Tom and Viv (1994) starring Willem Dafoe as TS Eliot
Oldies but goodies:	Accident (1967) starring Stanley Baker and Dirk Bogarde
	Arabesque (1966) starring Gregory Peck and Sophia Loren
	The Titfield Thunderbolt (1953) starring Stanley Holloway and a train
Cameo roles:	New College in the 1997 Bond movie Tomorrow Never Dies
	St. Thomas' Street in A Fish Called Wanda (1988)
	Oxford Castle in 102 Dalmatians (2000)
Best supporting actor:	Magdalen College was featured in Accident, Wilde, Shadowlands and Howard's End.
Not a lot of people know that:	Oxford doubled for Harvard in Heaven's Gate (1981), Michael Cimino's infamous studio-bankrupting historical saga.
Behind the scenes:	Oxford University and City Tour: daily from the Oxford Information Centre at 11.00am and 2.00pm, with extra tours at busy times. £6.00 per adult, £3.00 per child. ✆ 01865 726871

STEPHEN FRY AND JUDE LAW BRINGING OSCAR WILDE AND LORD ALFRED DOUGLAS TO LIFE IN WILDE (1997) ▶

On Location Harry Potter

The movies:	Harry Potter and the Sorcerer's Stone (2001)
	Harry Potter and the Chamber of Secrets (2002)
	Harry Potter and the Goblet of Fire (2005)
The locations:	Christ Church College, Oxford.
	Divinity School, Bodleian Library, Oxford.
	Duke Humfrey's Library, Bodleian Library, Oxford.
The scenes:	Christ Church College's dining hall is used as Hogwarts dining hall. The building features a distinctive hammerbeam roof and was built in the 1500s, but was updated with battlements and pinnacles in the 19th century.
	The Divinity School is used as Hogwarts Sanatorium. The ceiling features images of beasts and biblical scenes, and is a classic of English Gothic architecture. Built in 1488, it is normally used for the teaching of theology at Oxford University.
	Duke Humfrey's Library doubles as Hogwarts Library. With more than 80 miles of book shelves, it is one of the most complete libraries in the world.
Did you know?	Tourism to Oxford has risen by around 40% purely because of the Harry Potter movies.
	Christ Church is Oxford's largest college, and the only college in the world with a cathedral within its walls. It previously served as the inspiration for Lewis Carroll while writing Alice's Adventures in Wonderland.
Behind the scenes:	Christ Church is open to the public most days of the year (Monday to Saturday 9am-5pm, Sunday 1pm-5pm).
	Visitors are welcome at the Divinity School. Times vary. Telephone for details.
	Duke Humfrey's Library Term Hours: Mon-Fri 9.00-22.00, Sat 9.00-13.00 Vacation Hours: Mon-Fri 9.00-19.00, Sat 9.00-13.00 Closed Periods: Christmas Eve to New Year's Day, Good Friday to Easter Monday, Encaenia, August Bank Holiday weekend.
Get in touch	Christ Church College ✆ 01865 276150
	Bodleian Library ✆ 01865 277000

◄ THE DINING HALL AT CHRIST CHURCH COLLEGE

On Location: Inspector Morse

The TV series:	Inspector Morse – ITV (1987 – 2000)
The stories:	Adapted from the books by Colin Dexter. Lugubrious detective Inspector Morse (John Thaw) and the faithful Sergeant Lewis (Kevin Whately) solve murders in and around the normally peaceful settings of Oxford.
The series:	One of the milestones of British television, winning six BAFTAs. A launchpad for the directing careers of Danny Boyle (Trainspotting) and John Madden (Shakespeare In Love). Writers included Julian Mitchell (Wilde) and Anthony Minghella (The English Patient).
The filming:	Dozens of locations throughout Oxfordshire. Did for the county's tourism industry what Bergerac did for Jersey.
The locations:	Mainly in Oxford, but also featuring Woodstock, Didcot, Watlington and Henley.
Colleges:	Brasenose, University, Wadham, Christ Church, Magdalen, Exeter, New, Oriel, Pembroke, Merton.
Public buildings:	Ashmolean Museum, Covered Market, Oxford Town Hall, Pitt Rivers Museum, Sheldonian Theatre, Blackwell's Bookshop.
Hotels and pubs:	The Randolph Hotel, The Eagle and Child, The Turf Tavern and The Bear Inn (all Oxford). Plus the Trout (Wolvercote) and The Black Prince and Woodstock Arms (both Woodstock).
Further afield:	Didcot Railway Centre, Wytham Woods, Shirburn Castle (Watlington) and the Oxford Canal.
Missing locations:	Lonsdale College does not exist – it was modelled on Brasenose.
	Brakspear's Brewery in Henley is now the Hotel du Vin.
Did you know?	The best book-of-the-series is Inspector Morse Country by Cliff Goodwin.
Behind the scenes:	Inspector Morse Tours of Oxford. Saturdays only. Adults: £6.50, children £3.50. ✆ 01865 726871.

68

On Location: Brideshead Revisited

The TV series:	Brideshead Revisited – Granada TV (1981)
The locations:	Christ Church College, Oxford
	Wadham College, Oxford
	Hertford College, Oxford
The story:	Impoverished Charles Ryder (Jeremy Irons) comes under the spell of the dashing Sebastian Flyte (Anthony Andrews) whilst they are students at Oxford in the 1920s.
	Described by the novel's author, Evelyn Waugh, as "an attempt to trace the workings of the divine purpose in a pagan world."
The facts:	Back in the days when ITV used to make ground-breaking drama, Brideshead swept the board, winning seven BAFTAs, two Golden Globes and an Emmy.
	As well as launching the careers of its two main stars, the series also featured some of Britain's finest acting talent, including Laurence Olivier, John Gielgud and Claire Bloom.
	The novel was adapted for TV by John Mortimer, creator of Rumpole of the Bailey.
Did you know?	The semi-autobiographical tale was based on Waugh's experiences in Oxford as an undergraduate at Hertford College, where he came in 1922.
	A film version of the book is being made, with a screenplay by Andrew Davies (Pride and Prejudice, Bridget Jones) and starring Jude Law.
Behind the scenes:	Christ Church, on St Aldate's, is open daily. Tours cost £4. Advance booking is not required, except for special behind-the-scenes tours, for which an additional fee is payable. ✆ 01865 286573.
	Wadham College, on Parks Road, is open for free tours in term time (afternoons) and vacations (mornings and afternoons). Groups must book in advance. ✆ 01865 277900
	Hertford College, on Catte Street, is open daily for free tours. Maximum 10 people in a group. ✆ 01865 279400.

◀ JEREMY IRONS AND ANTHONY ANDREWS FILMING ON LOCATION IN OXFORD

Literary Landscapes Oxford

The preface	The university, together with Oxford's traditional role as a publishing centre, have combined to give the city an unrivalled literary reputation.
The students	Writers influenced by their time at Oxford include Middle East scholar and soldier TE Lawrence (The Seven Pillars of Wisdom), Kingsley Amis (the autobiographical Lucky Jim), and poet Matthew Arnold, who coined the term "dreaming spires."
The dons	Lord of the Rings creator JRR Tolkien was a professor at both Pembroke and Merton colleges.
	As Lewis Carroll, Christ Church mathematician Charles Dodgson created the immortal Alice's Adventures in Wonderland.
	Magdalen tutor CS Lewis told the story of his real-life love affair with American Joy Gresham in Shadowlands.
The drop-outs	Shelley came to study at University College in 1810 but was expelled in his first year.
	Samuel Johnson left Pembroke College after a year due to lack of funds.
The residents	Graham Greene and Ian Fleming both lived in Oxford for many years. Philip Pullman (His Dark Materials), Brian Aldiss (AI), John Bayley (Elegy for Iris) and Mark Haddon (The Curious Incident of the Dog in the Night-time) still do.
An Inspector Calls	Oxford and Colin Dexter's Inspector Morse are inseparable. The author lives in North Oxford.
	Aristocratic sleuth Lord Peter Wimsey, created by Somerville graduate Dorothy L Sayers, was a Balliol man.
	PD James, creator of Adam Dalgleish, was born in Oxford and still lives there.
Further afield	Garsington Manor, just outside Oxford, was a favourite gathering place of writers, including the Bloomsbury set, in the 1920s. Visitors included Virginia Woolf, Bertrand Russell and Aldous Huxley.
	Iris Murdoch lived in Steeple Aston near Bicester for 30 years before moving back to Oxford near the end of her life.
Literary walks	Blackwell's Bookshop organises a series of tours following in the footsteps of Tolkien, CS Lewis, Lewis Carroll, William Golding and others.
	✆ 01865 333696

THE LION, THE WITCH AND THE WARDROBE BY CS LEWIS HAS ENCHANTED GENERATIONS OF CHILDREN. TILDA SWINTON ▶ STARS IN THE LATEST FILM VERSION (2005)

Creation Theatre Company Oxford

Essentials

What is it?	Shakespeare in the park - and the tent.
Where is it?	Headington Hill Park in summer and the BMW Mirror Tent (Spielgeltent) in Oxford in winter.
Tell me more	The summer productions are held in an enclosed area of parkland, using natural backdrops and minimal props. The velvet canopies, mirrored roof and ornate pillars of the Spielgeltent form a spectacular setting for the winter shows.
The idea	Bringing Shakespeare to a wider audience.
What can I see?	Some of the Bard's most popular plays. Previous productions have included A Midsummer Night's Dream, As You Like It, Hamlet, Twelfth Night, and Romeo & Juliet.
Is it just Shakespeare?	No. Christmas shows have included A Christmas Carol.
Suitable for children?	Yes, for ten-year olds upwards. Creation prove that Shakespeare can be fun: open-air theatre at its best, entertaining and very funny.
Cost	Matinee prices from £8.50, evenings from £11 to £19.50.
Special offers	BMW sponsor the Theatre For A Fiver promotion for first-timers, with seats at £5 for anyone under 26.
What makes it special?	Shows that Shakespeare doesn't have to be stuffy. Why couldn't A Levels be like this?
Get in touch	✆ 01865 245745 www.creationtheatre.co.uk

Gossip & Secrets

Food and drink options	Crepes from on-site French chef Michel Sadones. Pimm's tent, plus wine and soft drinks. No picnics allowed.
Why is it so good?	Hugely entertaining, supremely talented professional actors.
Why is it not so good?	Seats are a touch hard, and open-air theatre is always a gamble, weather-wise. Cushions and rugs are available for hire however.
When to go	The summer season runs from June to August, the winter season from November to January. Check for dates.
In the know	Don't book expensive front-row seats: you can see from anywhere.

LOCATION SCOUT: PAUL ROUSE

A MIDSUMMER NIGHT'S DREAM STARRING DARREN ORMANDY AND STEPHANIE JORY ▶

Oxford Playhouse Oxford

Gossip & Secrets

What is it?	Oxfordshire's foremost theatre, presenting a fantastic variety of entertaining and original stage events – a full spectrum of plays, classic and contemporary dance and music, revues and talks – throughout the year. Brings in shows from all over the world as well as generating own productions.
Where is it?	In the heart of the city, opposite the Ashmolean. A short walk from the train and bus stations.
Cost	Ticket prices vary with performance, but typically:
	Adults: £17
	OAP's and children: £2 discount
	Students: £7 on the day
What makes it special?	Large enough to attract West End shows in rep, yet small enough to create intense and intimate theatrical atmosphere. Programme offers a feast of variety – 60-80 different shows in a year.
Best bit?	For theatre buffs, the post-show talks with the director and actors. For kids, the Playhouse's own annual Christmas panto. For me, the Autumn 2005 production of The Importance of Being Earnest, proving how to breathe new life into a familiar classic.
Food options	Two licensed bars offering full range of drinks, with sandwiches and pastries.
Got to see/do	Exciting holiday workshops for children from ages 9 to 18. Platform Performances with leading writers, actors, scientists, etc.
Get in touch	11-12 Beaumont Street Oxford OX1 2LW ✆ 01865 305305 (box office) www.oxfordplayhouse.com

LOCATION SCOUT: PAUL ROUSE

▼ TREADING THE BOARDS: DAVID SUCHET, SHEILA HANCOCK, WARREN MITCHELL AND STEPHANIE BEACHAM

Pegasus Theatre Oxford

Gossip & Secrets

What is it?	A small—scale vibrant theatre that presents a host of work from the UK and abroad, as well as home grown professional and amateur youth productions.
Where is it?	In East Oxford, 2 miles from the centre and easily accessible by bus and car.
Cost	Generally £8 max, but generous discounts for children and a range of other concessions available.
What makes it special?	A chance to see great work up close, in a friendly and intimate setting. Drama, dance, physical theatre, work for children and community projects.
Best bit?	The huge variety of work and affordable prices.
Food options	Fairtrade and organic snacks and drinks.
Got to see/do	A chance to join in with a whole range of workshops, classes and drama groups. No experience necessary for lots of the participatory work, and all age ranges catered for.
Get in touch	Magdalen Road Oxford OX4 1RE ✆ 01865 722851 www.pegasustheatre.org.uk

LOCATION SCOUT: MICHELLE DICKSON

Oxford's oldest **new quarter**

Oxford Castle is under siege once more – this time from people out to have fun.

Oxford Castle Limited
Estate Management Office
The Treadwheel Building
43 Oxford Castle Oxford OX1 1AY
www.oxfordcastle.com

bustling, cosmopolitan European-style piazzas. In an extraordinary development process that has seen bodies uncovered from the late Saxon period onwards and a wall believed to date from the 11th century, the accompanying archaeological dig and its amazing discoveries have been hot topics of conversation in Oxford for some time as the new project has unfolded.

So new in fact that, as we went to press, several of the establishments were just opening, giving a flavour of the fantastic Oxford Castle experience. Now there is something new for the city to talk about!

CAPTIVE AUDIENCE

Central to the site is a Malmaison Hotel, part of the super chic boutique hotel chain. It has added a new dimension to Oxford's city centre hotels. The company brings with it a reputation for excellence and creating hotels that are both comfortable and exciting, with a devoted following. With 94 rooms, you can now check into your very own "prison cell", clang shut the old prison door, and be locked up for the night in unabashed luxury.

Creating a destination all of its own, Oxford Castle is quickly becoming the place to be seen in Oxford. With eight restaurants to choose from, and an atmosphere reminiscent of lazy days in street cafes in southern Europe, you could almost forget you are in one of the world's most famous university cities, until you are reminded by the dramatic architecture of your surroundings, or realise that the person sitting at the next table is taking a welcome break from poring over text books by studying a menu instead.

And the choice is a wide one. In addition to the Malmaison brasserie and bar, famous brand names include Tootsies, La Tasca, Carluccios, Prezzo, PizzaExpress, The Living Room and the Ha!Ha! Bar & Canteen, plus Krispy Kreme doughnuts.

How do you combine almost a thousand years of history with a contemporary leisure experience? Not easily, if you talk to anyone who has been involved in the regeneration of the Oxford Castle site.

But it has been done, in great style.

Situated on five acres of prime real estate right in the heart of the city, the Castle site has been home to prisoners, kings, sheriffs and film stars. Originally built for William the Conqueror, it has laid its footprints in history with hangings, royal scandals and medieval punishments. In more modern times, it was a rather unpleasant three-to-a-cell prison, and its bleakness has also been used as a backdrop for Hollywood blockbusters like 102 Dalmatians and Spy Game.

Now, for the first time, the site exists purely for pleasure.

In a unique partnership between Oxfordshire County Council and developers The Osborne Group, the whole site has been redeveloped into a series of

Food and drink is not the sole purpose of the pedestrian-only site however.

Why not visit "Oxford Castle Unlocked," the key to the heritage of the site, and indulge in a little history? Climb the Castle mound or enjoy the views from the top of St George's Tower. For those needing a shot of culture, how about O3, the unique round art gallery, featuring and celebrating award-winning Oxfordshire artists with a fresh exhibition every month. For those keen to practice the art of shopping, Oxford Castle also has several markets each week focusing on books, food, arts, crafts and antiques, with market days changing according to the seasons, and street theatre to entertain you whilst you shop, drink or dine.

Who said history was boring? ﬆ

CLASSIC LOCATiONS — HIDDEN SECRETS

ESSENTiALS

Run by Jean Pierre Morilleau (General Manager) and Alison Drummond (Estate Manager) of Oxford Castle Limited.

How big All numbers include outdoor seating areas: Malmaison (94 bedrooms; 110 covers in brasserie & bar); Tootsies (244); La Tasca (150); Carluccios (126); Prezzo (114); PizzaExpress (144); The Living Room (350 capacity bar, 178 covers in restaurant); Ha!Ha! (335).

How much Check websites for individual menus.

Children Welcome throughout. Oxford Castle Unlocked, the heritage interpretation centre (opening Easter 2006), includes an education centre specifically aimed at children – venture underground or be locked in a cell!

Where is it There are four entrances to the site from: Paradise Street, New Road, Castle Street and Tidmarsh Lane.

Get in touch/visit Oxford Castle Limited
Estate Management Office
The Treadwheel Building
43 Oxford Castle Oxford OX1 1AY
www.oxfordcastle.com

81

GOSSiP & SECRETS

Malmaison Crafted out of the old prison buildings, with cells converted into luxury bedrooms. Metal staircases and other prison architecture intact. Rooms from £140 per night. 94 bedrooms, brasserie and bar.
www.malmaison.com

The Living Room Super cool restaurant and piano bar with a private members' room, The Study. This is a place to be seen in!
www.thelivingroom.co.uk

Prezzo Part of the south of England chain of stylish minimalist Italian restaurants, known for their fresh food and choice of wines.
www.prezzoplc.co.uk

Tootsies Will make you feel instantly at home: contemporary dining with a twist and not to be missed.
www.tootsiesrestaurants.co.uk

La Tasca Sunny Spain comes to Oxford. Tapas, paella, and a wide range of Spanish wines and beers.
www.latasca.co.uk

Carluccios Contemporary Italian caffé, food shop and deli, courtesy of acclaimed author and cook Antonio Carluccio. Simple, genuine food, using the freshest Italian ingredients..
www.carluccios.com

PizzaExpress Needs no introduction. The first and still the best, founded in 1965..
www.pizzaexpress.co.uk

Ha! Ha! Bar and canteen, specialising in American-style food, especially burgers and brunch. Fun for kids. Sells its own range of merchandise, from aprons to hampers.
www.hahaonline.co.uk

Krispy Kreme Doughnuts Doughnuts, cheesecake and hot & cold drinks.
www.krispykreme.co.uk

LOCATION PARTNER

The visual arts Oxford

Gossip & Secrets

Behind the scenes	One of Oxford's quirks is the way it hides its cultural activity. But a little time spent hunting will reveal an extraordinary richness of work in every media from traditional fine art and craft to contemporary arts.
Where?	You won't find many of the smallest venues in any guidebooks — except this one. Be sure to check what's on, and when, carefully.
Artweeks	An annual celebration — from mid May to early June — of Oxford's active and varied art scene. Open studios with artists and craftspeople displaying work in every media. The only way to tackle the festival is by a careful trawl through the guide with its maps — preferably in the excellent cafes at the Ashmolean Museum or Modern Art Oxford. Also available from Tourist Information Centres, the Town Hall, libraries and many shops.
Local artists	Many of the spaces listed in the Artweeks guide also display work throughout the year, usually of local or regional artists. See what's on at the Said Business School, Wolfson College, The Stables Gallery at Green College or the Jacqueline du Pre Building at St Hilda's College. St Edwards School hosts one of the country's leading ceramic fairs in November, and the expanding art centre has an increasingly ambitious range of exhibitions.
Co–operative spaces	Work by local artists can also be seen at Magdalen Road Studios, St. Mary's workshops and The Oxford Printmakers Workshop, either by appointment or during Artweeks. Occasional shows run at other times in the year.
Students	The Ruskin School of Drawing and Oxford Brookes University mount shows of graduating students' work in June. Expect to find students exploring the nature of art in every media — sometimes challenging, sometimes banal, sometimes exquisitely made. Oxford Brookes also mounts occasional shows at its Richard Hamilton Building and the Old Dairy, both on Headington Hill.
Elsewhere	Regular art and craft fairs take place at such venues as Blenheim Palace near Woodstock and Fawley Court near Henley.
Get in touch	See our venues listing on the following pages.

LOCATION SCOUT: ALAN BERMAN

ARTIST SARAH NORVILLE ON SHOW AT FAWLEY COURT ▶

The Ashmolean	One of the country's finest collections, housing world-class art and artifacts, ancient and modern. Fabulous range of work in comfortably sized rooms which you may often have to yourself. For instant immersion, go straight to the first floor for exceptional works by Ucello, Tura, Titian, Dutch and Flemish Masters, a fabulous Sisley collection, other Impressionists, and fine examples of English moderns such as Nash and Wood.
	The Museum also mounts wonderful temporary exhibitions such as Chinese Painting, Botanical Illustration and Early Italian Prints.
Christ Church Picture Gallery	Literally buried underground in the heart of Christ Church College, it displays an exquisite collection of medieval and classical paintings and drawings, and mounts a programme of shows of mainly drawings and small works. One of Oxford's gems in one of Britain's finest post-war buildings, by architects Powell and Moya.
Methodist Collection of Christian Art	Housed at Oxford Brookes University's Institute of Education, this small but high quality collection includes pre-Raphaelite works, plus pieces by Graham Sutherland, Eric Gill, Elizabeth Frink and Edward Burra. By appointment only, as the work is often on tour.
Highly recommended	Modern Art Oxford, OVADA and Pitt Rivers Museum (see reviews).

Gallery guide		
	Artweeks	✆ 01865 861574
	Ashmolean Museum	✆ 01865 278018
	Christ Church Picture Gallery	✆ 01865 276172
	Jacqueline du Pre Building	✆ 01865 276884
	Magdalen Road Studios	✆ 01865 730110
	Oxford Brookes University	✆ 01865 741111
	Oxford Printmakers Workshops	✆ 01865 726472
	Ruskin College	✆ 01865 554331
	Said Business School	✆ 01865 288800
	St. Edwards School	✆ 01865 319204
	St. Mary's Workshops	✆ 01865 722429
	Stables Gallery (Green College)	✆ 01865 274770
	Wolfson College	✆ 01865 274100

Out of town		
	Blenheim Palace, Woodstock	✆ 08700 602080
	Bohun Gallery, Henley	✆ 01491 576228
	Brian Sinfield Gallery, Burford	✆ 01993 824464
	Fawley Court, Henley	✆ 01491 574917

LOCATION SCOUTS: ALAN BERMAN, PAUL ROUSE

◄ ART ON SHOW IN OXFORDSHIRE, INCLUDING EXAMPLES FROM THE ASHMOLEAN (TOP LEFT) AND ARTWEEKS.

Modern Art Oxford

Gossip & Secrets

What is it?	Gallery showing contemporary visual art, often with film, music, poetry and other cultural events. Closed Mondays.
Where is it?	Next to the Royal Blenheim Pub on the corner of St Ebbe's Street and Pembroke Street. Five minutes walk from Gloucester Green bus station. Multi-storey parking in nearby Westgate Shopping Centre. Disabled parking on St Ebbe's Street.
Cost	Free entrance, but booking or ticket purchase required for some events. See website for details.
What makes it special?	Full of surprises. Approachable but very busy director and staff. Exciting shows, lovely meeting place, bookshop, licensed bar, Art Trolley for children accompanied by an adult at weekends — some late evenings.
Best bit?	Small entrance concealing vast upper galleries.
Food options	Delicious hot and cold freshly made food, salad, soup, quiches, etc. Children's menu and portions at half-price. Licensed bar.
Got to see/do	Varied and interesting exhibitions, lively debates, friendly gatherings, imaginative educational programme and many courses — practical and theoretical — for all ages and levels of expertise.
	MAO not only shows the work of international stars in the art world but also draws on members of the Oxford academic world, artists and art students from the region, and the vibrant multicultural communities of the city itself to enrich its exhibitions and activities.
Get in touch	30 Pembroke Street Oxford OX1 1BP ✆ 01865 722733 www.modernartoxford.org.uk

LOCATION SCOUT: HELEN GANLY

OVADA Oxford

Gossip & Secrets

What is it?	Gallery space presenting monthly exhibitions of contemporary art by artists based in Oxfordshire and the surrounding area.
Where is it?	Right inside Oxford's main Gloucester Green bus station.
Cost	Free admission.
What makes it special?	Partly the location, a gallery in a bus station from which all the comings and goings on outside are visible, as well as the programme of exhibitions, which constantly changes and surprises.
Best bit?	Meeting local artists at the exhibition openings.
Got to see/do	Artist-led children's workshops on themes related to the exhibitions.
Get in touch	21 Gloucester Green Oxford OX1 2AQ
	✆ 01865 201782
	www.ovada.org.uk

LOCATION SCOUT: KIRSTY BRACKENRIDGE

Artweeks

Essentials

What is it?	Oxfordshire's largest visual arts festival. Hundreds of artists across the county open up their homes and invite the public in.
Where is it?	Across Oxfordshire in May/June.
Cost	Free.
What makes it special?	Artweeks does make ordinary life seem that much more remarkable, that all this art is bubbling away behind the ordinary house-fronts of Oxford.
Best bit?	Best of all, I think, was an exhibition in 2005 by a six year-old boy, who lives across the street. He spent a whole day pinning up his drawings and paintings in his hallway, and made a hand-made 'Artweeks' flag which he put outside his house and opened the door for the public. This is the real spirit of Artweeks.
Get in touch	PO Box 281 Oxford OX2 9FX
	✆ 01865 861574
	www.artweeks.org

LOCATION SCOUT: TED DEWAN

▲ GREEN FINGERS: THE BOTANIC GARDEN IS THE COUNTRY'S OLDEST

Botanic Garden Oxford

Essentials

Full name	The University of Oxford Botanic Garden
What is it?	The UK's oldest botanic garden, dating from 1633.
Where is it?	In Rose Lane, bounded by the River Cherwell and Christchurch Meadow. Accessible from the High Street.
Cost	Adults – £2.60. Children free if accompanied by an adult.
What makes it special?	Mature walled garden with fountain, ponds, historic trees and botanical family borders; glasshouses burgeoning with lush tropical greenery. A colourful textured space for relaxation and contemplation throughout the year.
Best bit?	The Lily House with its huge Victoria water lilies in summer; the steamy exoticism of the Palm House in winter; the Insectivorous House and its voracious inhabitants all year round.
Got to see/do	Evening lectures, children's trails, school programmes.
Get in touch	Rose Lane Oxford OX1 4AZ ✆ 01865 286690 www.botanic-garden.ox.ac.uk

LOCATION SCOUT: LINDA MOWAT

Museum of Natural History Oxford

Gossip & Secrets

Full name	University of Oxford Museum of Natural History.
What is it?	A large and varied collection of minerals, fossils, insects and animals, including dinosaurs and a dodo.
Where is it?	Parks Road, close to Keble College.
Cost	Free.
What makes it special?	As well as containing fascinating skeletons, fossils, model dinosaurs, live bees and cockroaches, it is housed in a stunning Victorian building with a glass roof and galleries overlooking the main exhibition. The museum has become increasingly family-friendly, resulting in the richly-deserved Guardian Family Friendly award in 2005.
Best bit?	The museum is full of surprises, and each visit reveals another intriguing element. I particularly like the small pillars on each floor, each made from a different rock from the UK.
Food options	None.
Got to see/do	Try the Family Backpacks which are available on a Sunday, don't miss upstairs, and look out for another fascinating museum, the Pitt Rivers Museum, which can be reached via a door at the back.
When is it open?	Daily 12pm - 5pm
Get in touch	South Parks Road, Oxford OX1 3PP ✆ 01865 272950 www.oum.ox.ac.uk

Pitt Rivers Museum Oxford

Gossip & Secrets

What is it?	Vast collection of anthropological and archaeological artefacts collected by travellers, missionaries, anthropologists and scholars.
What makes it special?	Unique Victorian displays combined with modern interpretation.
Got to see/do	Don't miss the rituals/beliefs and textiles collections.
When is it open?	Daily 12pm - 4.30pm

LOCATION SCOUT: MIKE DENNIS

Oxford Contemporary Music

Essentials

What is it?	The most innovative New Music promoter/commissioning body in the south of England. Their annual programme features over 30 unique events ranging from art rock and free jazz to music theatre, world music, film installations and contemporary classical music.
Where is it?	At venues across Oxford, including intimate rooms for a small audience of 70, larger halls for up to 900, and spaces which have never embraced musical performance before.
Cost	Generally: £13.50 (£9 concessions)
What makes it special?	The restless and pioneering spirit which informs their imaginative commissioning of new work and programming. You never know what to expect or how and where the music will be presented.
Best bit?	Whatever you go and see in the OCM programme, you know it's going to be fascinating, inspirational and unique..
Got to see/do	Catch one of their sound/light/pyrotechnic fantasias in the Oxford University Botanic Garden.
Get in touch	Westminster Institute of Education Harcourt Hill Oxford OX2 9AT ✆ 01865 488369 www.ocmevents.org

LOCATION SCOUT: MAX REINHARDT

Music at Oxford

What is it?	Independent classical music promoter.
Where is it?	Venues vary according to concert.
Cost	From £10 to £37.
What makes it special?	Listening to world-class musicians performing in beautiful and historic buildings in Oxford.
Best bit?	Amazing artists, accessible programmes, beautiful venues.
Got to see/do	Join their mailing list to get details of rising young stars.
Get in touch	10b Littlegate Oxford OX1 1QTT ✆ 0870 7500659 www.musicatoxford.com

LOCATION SCOUT: CLARE SALTER

CHLOE HANSLIP IS AMONG THE MANY TALENTED CLASSICAL MUSICIANS WHO HAVE PLAYED IN OXFORD ▶

Cowley Road Carnival Oxford

Essentials

What is it?	Biggest multi-cultural community event in Oxfordshire. Mini-Notting Hill with procession, dance and music stages, street entertainment and food produce from every continent.
Where is it?	Cowley Road and adjoining streets, in East Oxford.
Cost	Free to all.
What makes it special?	A huge celebration of the diverse cultural make-up of East Oxford. Fantastic mix of music/dance and performances – a spectacular procession. Local cafes/restaurants and stalls selling delicious food from all over the world. Everyone is welcomed and it feels like one big party.
Best bit?	Walking from one end of the road to the other and on the way sampling a distinctive smell, sound, sight or taste that transports you from one evocative cultural experience to another.
Food options	Take your pick – within this one road you can choose from Indian, Caribbean, Polish, Italian, Thai, Chinese, French or whatever food you can think of to indulge in.
In the know	It's only held once a year in June – so make sure you're in Oxford to start with. Be on time to see the procession – it's full of variety with wonderful costumes, cute children, samba bands and acrobatic Chinese dragons, but most of all a huge cultural melting pot of faces and people celebrating and enjoying this annual street party.
Get in touch	Henrietta Gill (Carnival Co-ordinator) East Oxford Action ✆ 01865 200780 www.eastoxford.com

LOCATION SCOUT: YASMIN SIDHWA

◄ COLOURFUL SCENES AT THE COWLEY ROAD CARNIVAL

An Ideal Day Out Oxford

Why Oxford?	The perfect city for exploring on foot or by bicycle – especially in the summer.
Breakfast	In the Covered Market, at Mortons, Browns or Brothers. I have spent many happy hours – and added many pounds! – here. The market has a superb range of food, clothes, flowers, shoes and interesting pictures and jewellery.
Morning glory	Out of the market onto the High Street and down the narrow passage past Gill's the Ironmongers and the Wheatsheaf to Blue Boar Street. Turn left past the Bear pub – famous for its collection of ties – into Oriel Place and then cut in between Corpus and Merton into Christ Church Meadow.
Fresh air	The full circuit of the Meadow is 1.2 miles, taking you along the Thames and the Cherwell. If that's too daunting, turn left and walk along Dead Man's Walk to the Botanic Garden – Britain's oldest. A beautiful and tranquil place.
Lunch	From the Botanic Garden, turn right and stop for lunch at Café Coco or the Kasbar in the Cowley Road, or Fishers or Moya in St Clements; or turn left for the rococo splendour of the Grand Café in the High Street. And don't miss out on a visit to Magdalen College.
Culture vultures	University Parks to watch cricket, then time for a quick peek at the dinosaurs in the Natural History Museum or the treasures of the Pitt Rivers Museum.
Tea	Cream tea in The Old Parsonage or Brown's, or a pint of excellent Young's beer at the King's Arms next to Wadham College or the Turf Tavern hidden away behind Holywell.
Dinner	Quod Bar in the Old Bank Building in the High. Get a table near the windows and watch the evening draw on and the world pass by. Good brasserie food and choose from a wide range of interesting wines.

LOCATION SCOUT: BOB PRICE, LORD MAYOR OF OXFORD

◀ OXFORD SIGHTS (CLOCKWISE FROM TOP LEFT): BOB PRICE GETS ON HIS BIKE; THE RADCLIFFE CAMERA; THE BOTANIC GARDEN; THE BRIDGE OF SIGHS; QUOD; THE HIGH STREET

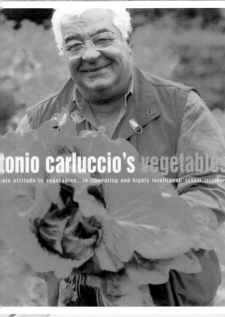

An Ideal Day Out North Oxfordshire

Teeing off	A steaming cup of coffee and a sausage & egg sandwich for breakfast at Rye Hill Golf Club, followed by 18 holes of golf on a championship length course which overlooks some of North Oxfordshire's finest countryside.
Liquid refreshment	A short drive for lunch at the Saye & Sele Arms in Broughton. The owners of the pub, Danny and Liz McGeehan, are accomplished chefs in their own right. Danny's homemade pies are to die for, and all of his desserts are made on the premises.
Movie magic	After lunch and a decent pint, a short walk to Broughton Castle, a picturesque manor house with a substantial moat. It has featured in numerous movies, including Shakespeare in Love and The Madness of King George, and for those of you who are able to remember, the Morecambe & Wise Christmas Show 1975.
Spice of life	After a couple of hours at Broughton Castle, walking round the gardens and grounds, jump in the car for the short trip to Bloxham. A swift pint at the Joiners Arms before finishing up at the Spice of Bengal Indian restaurant in Deddington.
In my defence	Now before you accuse me of having eaten out on three occasions, I would like to remind you that I would have walked quite a long way round Rye Hill, and will have used up lots of energy thrashing my clubs at a little white ball. However, I should also point out that in addition to having one of the area's largest pro shops, Rye Hill do hire out electric golf buggies for those too lazy to walk.
Get in touch	Rye Hill Golf Club Milcombe OX15 4RU. ✆ 01295 721818.
	Broughton Castle Banbury OX15 5EB. ✆ 01295 722547.
	Saye & Sele Arms Main Road Broughton OX15 5ED. ✆ 01295 263348.
	Spice of Bengal New Street Deddington OX15 0SP. ✆ 01869 337733.

LOCATION SCOUT: SHAUN JARDINE

◄ FURTHER AFIELD IN NORTH OXFORDSHIRE: (CLOCKWISE FROM TOP LEFT) THE SIR CHARLES NAPIER IN CHINNOR; HISTORIC BANBURY; FLYING HIGH NEAR ENSTONE; CARLUCCIOS AT BICESTER VILLAGE; HOOK NORTON

Carluccios Bicester

Gossip & Secrets

The food	Fresh, tasty, modern Italian with style.
The drink	Good cross-section of Italian whites and reds, plus Italian beer.
Why is it so good?	Informal dining at its best. Recipes created by founder Antonio Carluccio. Superb deli counter with products you won't find anywhere else in Oxfordshire.
To die for	On the menu – cassata, a Sicilian ice cream dessert.
	At the deli – just about everything!
Occasions	Lunchtime shopping break. Also open evenings.
Atmosphere	Noisy, buzzing. Minimalist Italian trattoria.
In the know	You can't book a table, so get there for an early lunch to avoid the queues.

Essentials

Run by	Manager Karen Westfield. Part of the national chain.
How big?	100 covers.
Where is it?	Close to West Gate entrance of Bicester Village shopping outlet.
How much?	Antipasti from £4.15 to £6.25
	Mains from £5.95 to £10.95
	Desserts from £3.95 to £5.25
	Wines from £10.95 to £23
When is it open?	Daily 9am-10pm.
Get in touch	Bicester Village OX26 6WD
	✆ 01869 247651
	www.carluccios.com

LOCATION SCOUT: PAUL ROUSE

Sir Charles Napier Chinnor

Gossip & Secrets

The food	This 'pub' is more of a restaurant. Sophisticated, yet not overwhelming, with a changing menu and specials.
The drink	A real understanding of how to achieve a diverse selection of wines without breaking the bank. Champagne is on tap!
Why is it so good?	Relaxed, fabulous service, but still cosy and friendly. I always come away feeling pleasantly stuffed and contented, as if I had been to good friends for dinner.
Why is it not so good?	The bar area is small and can feel overcrowded if everyone wants pre-dinner/lunch drinks.
To die for	The sculptures. Michael Cooper uses the restaurant and grounds as a showcase. (www.michaelcoopersculptor.com)
Occasions	Celebrations, birthday treats. Winter is warm and snug, summer has the fabulous gardens to sit and relax in.
In the know	Red Kites nest in the area, and provide afternoon aerial displays if you keep your eyes peeled.

Essentials

How big?	80 covers. Another 80 on the terrace in good weather.
Where is it?	South east of Thame, close to the M40.
How much?	Average starters £8; mains £15-£18; desserts £6.75.
When is it open?	Tuesday to Sunday Lunch: 12 – 2.30pm (3.30pm Sunday) Tuesday to Saturday Dinner: 7 – 10pm
Get in touch	Sprigg's Alley Nr. Chinnor OX39 4BX ✆ 01494 483011 www.sircharlesnapier.co.uk

LOCATION SCOUT: KATE ROUSE

Banbury House Hotel Banbury

Gossip & Secrets

The hotel	Well maintained with smart and attentive staff, keen to please. 63 rooms providing comfortable accommodation with prices reduced for weekend breaks to £48 per person B&B or £65 including dinner.
The restaurant	Pleasantly decorated and laid out. Warm and relaxed atmosphere with some thought for an appropriate level of privacy.
The food	Table d'hote menu with seven choices for each course, well prepared and presented.
The drink	Matches the expectations.
Why is it so good?	The management team closely monitor service standards and customer needs. Clear evidence of a willingness to please.
Why is it not so good?	The hotel is used regularly by tour operators/business groups, with independent guests sometimes relegated to smaller rooms.
Occasions	Passing through on longer journeys North/South, or weekend breaks. Also weddings/conferences/business meetings.
In the know	Conveniently placed as a stopover facility for long journeys or anyone visiting Blenheim Palace, Silverstone, Oxford and Stratford.
Don't just take our word for it	AA 3-star.

Essentials

Run by	Managed by Debbie Hinks. Part of Best Western.
How big?	63 rooms, conference facilities, bar and restaurant.
Where is it?	On the edge of the town within easy walking distance of the centre.
How much?	Weekdays £90, weekends £48 for B&B. Table d'hote menu £22 for 3 courses.
Get in touch	Oxford Road Banbury OX16 9AH
	✆ 01295 259361
	www.banburyhouse.co.uk

LOCATION SCOUT: BERNARD GOODCHILD

Deddington Arms Deddington

Gossip & Secrets

The food	Formal dining in a delightful dining room and a wide variety of bar meals. Great menu for Sunday lunch. Good steaks.
The drink	Pub prices, a good wine list, and a wide variety of wines by the glass.
Why is it so good?	Very friendly. The food is of a high standard and the hotel also offers a number of themed opera, jazz and fine dining events. Jamie Cullum played here before he was famous!
Why is it not so good?	Sometimes the bar area does get a little busy if there is a big sporting occasion, as the locals tend to congregate to watch TV.
To die for	Scallops with a leek and cream starter and rump of lamb with garlic and chive risotto.
Occasions	A quick evening meal in the bar if you can't be bothered to cook. Sunday lunches or special occasions in the restaurant.
When to go	Great at any time. Sunday lunches are popular – you need to book.
Atmosphere	Comfortable, nicely decorated. Well trained staff. Children welcome.
In the know	There is a lovely table in the bay window at the front of the restaurant. Deddington is a beautiful village with honey-coloured houses, and the Deddington Arms is at the heart of it. If you are feeling energetic, there are some wonderful circular walks – see the village website at www.deddington.org.uk
Don't just take our word for it	Good Pub Guide, AA Rosette Restaurant Guide, Britain's Best Country Pubs For Food Lovers, AA Hotel Guide.

Essentials

Run by	Paul Haverson – Manager. Part of a small privately-owned group of four hotels.
How big?	60 covers in restaurant and 20 in the bar.
How much?	Average starter £6; main £14; dessert £5.
When is it open?	Lunch and evening, seven days a week.
Get in touch	Horsefair Deddington OX15 0SH ∅ 01869 338364 www.deddington-arms-hotel.co.uk

LOCATION SCOUT: SHAUN JARDINE

Black Boy Milton

Gossip & Secrets

The food	Good pub grub. Sources local ingredients and cooks to a high standard.
The drink	Not tied to any particular brewery. Good choice of real ales and wines.
Why is it so good?	Relaxed atmosphere. Pleasant dining room. Lovely courtyard garden hidden away at the back of the pub.
Why is it not so good?	Small car park — but space can usually be found nearby.
To die for	Steaks, chicken curry, bread and olives.
Atmosphere	Laid back but professional. Nice areas to sit outside in summer.
In the know	Booking essential for Sunday lunches and advisable rest of the time.

Essentials

How big?	45 covers in restaurant. Also beer garden and play area.
Where is it?	Centre of village, just outside Bloxham.
How much?	Average starter £5; main £9.50; dessert £4.50.
When is it open?	Lunch and evening 7 days a week.
Get in touch	Milton Nr Banbury OX15 4HH
	✆ 01295 722111

LOCATION SCOUT: SHAUN JARDINE

Hook Norton

Essentials

What is it?	Not so much a village as THE place to discover the beer history of Oxfordshire.
Where is it?	Between Chipping Norton and Banbury.
Cost	The historic brewery offers two-hour tours including a tasting session and a free glass. Price: £8.50 for person.
What makes it special?	One of only 32 family run brewers left in the country and the only one to be still driven by steam.
Get in touch	www.hooknortonbrewery.co.uk

LOCATION SCOUT: KATE ROUSE

Great Western Arms Aynho

Gossip & Secrets

The food	Fantastic fish, good steaks and other classic dishes.
The drink	Reasonably priced. Local Hook Norton beer, extremely well kept. The pub also serves a huge selection of decent wine and champagne by the glass.
Why is it so good?	Incredibly relaxed atmosphere. This is a great gastro pub – most people go there to eat. Professional staff, excellent chef. The pub is located next to the Oxford Canal, so there are some delightful walks.
To die for	Seafood trio – calamari, whitebait and sardines. Classic fish and chips. Calves liver with onions.
When to go	Anytime. But booking is essential.
Atmosphere	Very comfortable. Roaring fires in the winter.
In the know	The best table in wintertime is the round table in the main body of the restaurant, next to the fire.
Don't just take our word for it	Good Pub Guide (in Northants section, as it's on the border).

Essentials

How big?	80 covers.
Where is it?	Adjacent to the Oxford Canal, in between Aynho and Deddington.
How much?	Average starter £6; average main course £11; average dessert £4.50.
When is it open?	Lunch and evenings 7 days a week, although closes Sunday evenings in wintertime.
Get in touch	Aynho Station Deddington OX17 3BP. ✆ 01869 338288

LOCATION SCOUT: DEBRA JARDINE

Bicester Village Bicester

Essentials

What is it?	Purpose-built Outlet retail village with tons of bargains. Just about every top brand name you can think of. Over 90 shops offering up to 60% off original prices. Sells women's, men's and children's fashion, sportswear, shoes, travel goods, jewellery, gifts, accessories, lingerie, home design goods and beauty products.
Style	Everything from Monsoon to Bally, Ozwald Boateng to Karen Millen, and Villeroy & Boch to The White Company. The Triumph shop is a must, as you can buy stylish undies for less than £20!
Size	Huge. This is a village in size as well as name, with modern New England-style shopping architecture.
What is so good about it?	Some good bargains, as it specialises in ends of lines, previous season's fashions, and seconds.
What is not so good about it?	All outdoor, which can be a pain when it rains. Can get very busy on Saturdays and bank holidays.
Food options	The ubiquitous Starbucks and Pret a Manger have thankfully been joined by Carluccios, so you know you can get a great meal, and make a full day of it.
In the know	Go online and sign up for the email newsletter, which keeps you up-to-date with news, offers and special events.
When is it open?	Seven days a week (except Christmas Day). Weekdays and Sundays 10am-6pm; Saturdays 9.30am-7pm. Some individual shops vary.
Where is it?	Take the M40 motorway to junction 9. Follow the A41 for 2 miles towards Bicester and signs to Bicester Village Outlet Centre.
Get in touch	Bicester Village 50 Pingle Drive Bicester OX26 6WD ✆ 01869 323 200 www.BicesterVillage.com

LOCATION SCOUT: KATE ROUSE

Farmers' Market Deddington

Where	The Market Place, Deddington.
When	Fourth Saturday of the month, 9.00am – 12.30pm.
What makes it special?	A real community affair, with locals helping put up and take down the covered stalls, selling their own goods, and adding to the chatter and buzz.
Atmosphere	Old-fashioned community spirit that turns a simple farmers' market into a social occasion.
Worth travelling for	Local meat, fresh fish, seasonal vegetables and fruit, traditional cakes, pies and pastries, free-range eggs, cheeses, ice cream, apple juice, wine, herbs and local crafts.
Not to be missed	Bakers' Basket – a sensational range of fresh bread from the traditional to the unusual. New recipes are always being introduced to tempt customers, so keep your eyes peeled!
In the know	Deddington is certified by the National Association of Farmers' Markets. This means the market can only sell goods that are locally produced, and that one of the principal producers or representatives must attend the market – so you really can chat to the farmer or producer.
Side shows	There's music as well. The market usually has a local street organ playing to add to the overall shopping experience.
Don't just take our word for it	Runner-up in the 2005 National Certified Market of the Year awards.
Get in touch	Charles Newey – chairman ✆ 01869 338282 charles.newey@deddington.net www.deddington.org.uk

LOCATION SCOUT: REBECCA DAWES

F Eagles Fresh Foods Deddington

Essentials

Style	Classic village version of the Harrods food hall.
Size	About 1500 sq ft. A large butchers, delicatessen and fishmongers combined, with an in-house chef who will happily cook fantastic meals in your own dishes – a great way to con people at dinner parties! The shop has dedicated areas dealing with fish, wine, home-cooked food, butchery, delicatessen, books, puddings and cakes.
Cost	Eagles supplies exceptionally high quality produce. As a result don't expect it to retail for similar amounts as the major supermarkets. Eagles watch word is "The taste must meet and exceed expectations." It does!
Exclusive stockists of:	Beef from Scotland.
	Lamb from England, Scotland and Wales.
	Pork and Bacon – UK reared.
	Poultry – from the West Country.
	Venison from Balmoral.
Get in touch	The Market Place Deddington near Banbury OX15 OSB. ✆ 01869 338500 www.feaglesfreshfoods.co.uk

LOCATION SCOUT: DEBRA JARDINE

3 Wishes Deddington

Essentials

Style	Ladies clothing.
Size	Small but perfectly formed.
Cost	Affordable designer label clothing.
Exclusive stockists of:	Betty Jackson, Joseph, Earl Jean and many more well-known names. Accessories and jewellery to match.
Get in touch	High Street Deddington Banbury OX15 OSJ. ✆ 01869 337415

LOCATION SCOUT: DEBRA JARDINE

Apples Cookery School Wardington

Essentials

What is it?	Where students, young and old, are given the opportunity to learn the basics of cooking and eating a healthy, balanced diet.
Where is it?	Village setting just outside Banbury, on the A361 to Daventry.
Cost	Single day course: £35 for 5-16 year olds. Three-day course: £99
	Adult prices vary according to type of course chosen. See website.
	Also caters for birthday parties, and organises social evenings, wine tasting and celebrity chef days. Gift vouchers available.
What makes it special?	Fun and friendly environment. After tuition, you create dishes on your own, giving you a feeling of independence.
Best bit?	Seeing the finished dish you have created all by yourself. Then eating it!
Food options	You cook your own lunch.
Got to see/do	Picking vegetables and herbs from the garden to use in your own recipes. Take home the recipe cards and try it again at home.
In the know	Courses run throughout the year. Produce used is seasonal and, where possible, local. All equipment is provided. For birthday parties, they supply party bags, birthday cakes and even a photographer as well as all the food.
Get in touch	Tuthill Park Wardington Nr Banbury OX17 1RY ✆ 01295 750720 www.applescookery.co.uk

LOCATION SCOUTS: HANNAH ENDACOTT (AGE 13) AND LUCY ENDACOTT (AGE 11)

A quick guide South Oxfordshire

Where is it?	Stretches from the M40 in the east almost to the M4 in the south, nudging the Chilterns, the Cotswolds and the Berkshire Downs.
Home Counties?	Not exactly, although people living in Henley-on-Thames tend to think of themselves as being in the Thames Valley rather than Oxfordshire.
Main towns	Henley-on-Thames — for art, music and rowing.
	Wallingford — for markets.
	Wantage — for churches, museums and the Uffington White Horse.
	Abingdon — for the Thames..
Picture postcard views	Sonning Common, Goring, Uffington, Clifton Hampden, Ewelme, Watlington, Dorchester, Letcombe Bassett.
Blot on the landscape	Didcot, and its infamous power station.
Historic houses	Mapledurham, Stonor, Fawley Court, Kingston Bagpuize.
Literary landscapes	Letcombe Bassett — Cresscombe in Jude The Obscure.
	Uffington — home to Thomas Hughes, creator of Tom Brown's Schooldays.
	Ewelme — home to Jerome K Jerome, author of Three Men in a Boat.
	Midsomer Murders — see separate review.
Must do	Pimms at Henley Regatta.
	Champagne at Henley Festival of Music.
	Pooh Sticks at Little Wittenham.
	Walking over Wittenham Clumps.
	Flying a kite on White Horse Hill.
	The Wind in the Willows exhibition at the River and Rowing Museum in Henley.

◄ OUT AND ABOUT IN SOUTH OXFORDSHIRE: KESTRELS AT FALLOWFIELDS; CRAFTS AT FAWLEY COURT; RODNEY BEWES MESSING ABOUT ON THE RIVER; WIND IN THE WILLOWS; AND CHAMPAGNE, FIREWORKS AND MUSICAL STARS — IL DIVO, VANESSA MAE AND KIRI TE KANAWA — AT THE HENLEY FESTIVAL OF MUSIC.

Le Manoir aux Quat' Saisons
Great Milton

Gossip & Secrets

The style	Entente cordiale – the perfect blend of England and France.
The food	The freshest – and best – ingredients, many from Le Manoir's own gardens. The inspiration of Raymond Blanc. And a superb brigade in the kitchen. You will go a long way to find a better restaurant.
The drink	Remarkable selection of wines from all over the world, chosen with the attention to detail evident everywhere. The wine list runs to over 40 pages – but the sommelier will advise.
Why is it so good?	Raymond Blanc's life, love and ongoing passion for over 20 years. Superb food and wine. Supremely efficient staff. Country house elegance without the pretension.
To die for	Almost anything on the menu. And the gardens – a foodie's idea of heaven. Wander around at your leisure.
Occasions	Special celebrations. Very romantic weekends. Very special clients.
Atmosphere	Relaxing. Unstuffy. And not a footballer's wife in sight.
In the know	The menu du jour, at £45 for three courses, is a cost-effective way of sampling the restaurant. The private dining room, with its own garden, is perfect for bigger celebrations or exclusive corporate events.
Don't just take our word for it	Two Michelin stars, and enough awards to fill a book on its own.

Essentials

Run by	Raymond Blanc at the helm, ably assisted by GM Tom Lewis.
How big?	Three restaurant areas, plus private dining facilities. 32 bedrooms.
Where is it?	Eight miles south east of Oxford.
How much?	Starters £30-£36; mains £36-£38; desserts £19. Wine from £22 to almost infinity. Rooms and suites from £360 to £1,250 per night.
When is it open?	Lunch: 12.15 pm to 2.30 pm. Dinner: 7.15 pm to 9.30 pm.
Get in touch	Church Road Great Milton OX44 7PD ✆ 01844 278881 www.manoir.com

LOCATION SCOUT: PAUL ROUSE

◀ LE MANOIR: RAYMOND BLANC'S PASSION SHOWS THROUGH

Milsoms Hotel & Loch Fyne Henley

Gossip & Secrets

The food	Superb selection of fresh fish and seafood – especially oysters, mussels, smoked salmon, kippers and Cromer crab.
The drink	Wide choice of whites and reds, from house wine at £6.75 to around £30.
Why is it so good?	Part of the Loch Fyne chain of 25 restaurants in the UK (including Oxford), with uniformly high standards. Milsoms, upstairs, is a delightful seven-room boutique hotel.
To die for	Kippers for breakfast, shellfish platter with crab for lunch..
When to go	Restaurant: anytime, including breakfast for non-residents. Hotel: romantic getaway, good-value business trips.
Atmosphere	Restaurant: usually busy, loud, buzzing. Hotel: a secluded haven.
In the know	Fish and seafood specials are excellent value. The fish and seafood counter sells fresh produce if you want to cook at home.
Don't just take our word for it	CEO Mark Derry was voted Group Restaurateur of the Year at the 2005 Caterer and Hotelkeeper awards.

Essentials

How big?	Restaurant: 180 covers Hotel: seven ensuite rooms
Where is it?	Central as it gets – in the market place
How much?	Restaurant: starters average £5.95, mains from £8.95 to £14.95, desserts from £3.95. Rooms: £75 per double room, with breakfast.
Get in touch	20 Market Place Henley-on-Thames RG9 2AH www.lochfyne.com www.milsomshotel.co.uk ✆ 01491 845780 (restaurant) ✆ 01491 845789 (hotel)

LOCATION SCOUT: PAUL ROUSE

White Hart Nettlebed

Gossip & Secrets

The food	Modern British cooking, with French influence. Imaginative seafood dishes. Order coffee to enjoy the best pistachio biscotti in England.
The drink	Good selection to suit all budgets. Expect to see good selection of Veuve Clicquot champagne.
Why is it so good?	The food. Plus the best small conference facilities in the area.
Why is it not so good?	In need of a good interior designer.
To die for	Pineapple carpaccio.
Occasions	Private and business functions for the more discerning customer.
When to go	Comes alive at the weekend.
Atmosphere	Laid back with air of calm professionalism.
In the know	Superb conference room, sponsored by Veuve Clicquot, with courtyard patio attached. Competitively priced and ample parking.
Don't just take our word for it	Top 50 Best Gastro Pubs in Britain – The Independent.

Essentials

Run by	Jean-Christophe Roumignac, or JC to those who know him.
How big?	12 bedrooms. Restaurant: 30 covers, Bistro: 60
Where is it?	On the main through road in Nettlebed, near Henley-on-Thames
How much?	Restaurant: 3-course table d'hote £35.00. Tasting Menu £55.00. Bistro: Average starter £4.95 Average main course £11.95 Average dessert £4.95 2-course Sunday lunch £12.95
When is it open?	Coffee, lunch & dinner – 7 days a week
Get in touch	Nettlebed Nr Henley-on-Thames RG9 5DD ✆ 01491 641245 www.whitehartnettlebed.com

LOCATION SCOUT: TRACEY JEFFERIES

The Himalayan Tandoori Henley

Gossip & Secrets

The food	Authentic Nepalese food. Specialises in Tandoori dishes and excellent selection of house specialities. Only fresh ingredients — all spices prepared in-house!
The drink	Tiger and Cobra beers plus selected wines..
Why is it so good?	Small, long-established restaurant run by Surya Yonjan and his family. Personal, friendly service. Helpful in-depth advice on dishes.
Why is it not so good?	No air-conditioning, so can get quite sticky in warm weather.
To die for	All the Tandoori dishes! Plus house specialities such as Chicken Tikka & Shaslick. The naan bread is superb.
Occasions	A great night out for small groups of friends, birthday parties, etc.
Atmosphere	Laid back and great fun.
In the know	Ask for a window seat and watch Henley go by. Small function room on the first floor.
Don't just take our word for it	Not in any of the main guides (which are often too snooty to include restaurants like this) but patronised by local celebrities including Rowan Atkinson and Nigel Havers.

Essentials

How big?	36 covers.
Where is it?	Centre of Henley — short walk from Greys Road car park.
How much?	Average starter — £3.00; main course — £6.95; dessert — £2.50. House wine: £9.50. Wine list averages £14-£15.
When is it open?	Lunch and dinner — seven days a week.
Get in touch	16 Reading Road Henley-on-Thames RG9 1AG.
	✆ 01491 410939
	www.thehimalayantandoori.co.uk

LOCATION SCOUT: SHEILA HAYLES

The Green Olive Henley

Gossip & Secrets

The food	Modern take on traditional Greek food, specialising in meze and lots of "sharing" dishes.
The drink	Wines by the glass and bottle — good choice of Greek wines and interesting selection from Spain, Italy and Chile. Large glass from £3.10, bottles from £12.00.
Why is it so good?	Cool decor. Lively atmosphere. Patio.
Why is it not so good?	Service can be a bit slow early in the week.
To die for	The House Special: a full set meze comprising over 22 dishes (hot and cold appetizers, grilled, baked & casserole dishes, and selection of Greek desserts). A challenge to eat it all!
Occasions	Celebrations with friends and family. A night out with the girls. Or couples looking for a reminder of their Mediterranean holidays.
When to go	Any time — but great at weekends. Very busy at Sunday lunch, so booking is always advised.
Atmosphere	Lively and light hearted. A place to relax.
In the know	The patio area seats 25-30. Great in summer, it can be pre-booked.

Essentials

Run by	Yannis Karakiuses — Manager. One other branch in Windsor.
How big?	80 covers in the main restaurant. Up to 30 on the patio.
Where is it?	As central as it gets — the Market Place in Henley. Two large car parks within two minutes walk.
How much?	Average starter: £3.95-£5.00. Average main course: £7.50-£8.00. Desserts: £4.25. Mini-Meze (10 + items) from £8.95. Full Set Meze (22 + items) from £21.95.
When is it open?	Lunch and dinner — seven days a week.
Get in touch	28 Market Place Henley-on-Thames RG9 2AH ℘ 01491 412220 www.green-olive.co.uk

LOCATION SCOUT: SHEILA HAYLES

Three Tuns Henley

Gossip & Secrets

The food	Upmarket pub food. Varies according to season but might include grilled Icelandic halibut with wild mushroom & sweet potato gnocchi, runner beans, borlotti beans & salsa verde; braised rabbit with baby onions, puy lentils and tarragon & mustard sauce; dark and white chocolate brownie with strawberry compote and creme fraiche ice cream.
The drink	Good selection of wine and beers.
Why is it so good?	Sophisticated contemporary cooking using local ingredients.
To die for	Any of their chocolate puddings!
When to go	Equally good for lunch or dinner.
Atmosphere	Eclectic surroundings and friendly atmosphere.
In the know	Ordinary frontage belies the good food inside.

Essentials

Where is it?	Bang in the centre of Henley, close to the Town Hall.
How much?	£30–35 per head with wine, dining à la carte. There is a £5 single course lunch option on Mondays – Fridays.
Get in touch	5 Market Place Henley-on-Thames RG9 2AA ✆ 01491 573260.

LOCATION SCOUT: RACHEL VINEY

Crooked Billet Stoke Row

Gossip & Secrets

The food	Really varied: Italian, French provincial and many popular brasserie favourites. Seafood is especially good. Menus changed regularly, offering plenty of choice. Extensive use of local produce.
The drink	Reasonably priced wine list, from both New World and Old World. Some excellent wines at the top end (£30-£40 a bottle).
Why is it so good?	The tucked away location and the sense of discovery as you arrive. The warm welcome from the staff and the pleasant feeling every time you settle yourself in front of the inglenook fireplace.
Why is it not so good?	Although an excellent restaurant, it is housed in a historic pub (1642) and is split into a series of cosy interconnecting rooms. Unlike other pubs, it therefore has no bar.
To die for	The jazz evenings are marvellous.
Occasions	Any special occasion, with family or friends. Plus business dinners.
Atmosphere	You walk in the door and go back in time.... particularly on a cold winter night. Yet the food is modern and sophisticated.
In the know	Be careful to request a table away from the door on a cold evening. The private dining room takes up to 50.
Don't just take our word for it	Good Food Guide, the Which Good Food Guide, the Good Pub Guide, AA Best Pubs & Inns Guide. Kate Winslet held her wedding reception here.

Essentials

How big?	70 covers.
Where is it?	Tucked away down a lane, away from the centre of the village.
How much?	Average starter £6.95; main course £15.70; dessert £5.50. Set Luncheon Menus from Monday to Saturday. Special Luncheon Menu available all day on Sundays.
When is it open?	Food served lunchtimes 12-2.15pm, evenings 7-10pm. All day on Sundays.
Get in touch	Newlands Lane Stoke Row RG9 5PU ✆ 01491 681048 www.thecrookedbillet.co.uk

LOCATION SCOUT: ANDREW RYAN

Bella Napoli Abingdon

Gossip & Secrets

The food	Traditional authentic Italian cuisine. Daily specials. Classic meat and fish dishes, fresh vegetables, regional specialities. Freshly made pizza and pasta. Home made desserts.
The drink	Extensive wine and drinks list including Neapolitan wines specially imported. Excellent fresh Italian coffee.
Why is it so good?	Family-run business with quality food in generous portions and relaxed surroundings. Friendly and knowledgeable staff, only too willing to inform you of the daily specials. More than your average pasta shop.
To die for	Sauces and pasta all homemade, and a sweet trolley from heaven.
Occasions	From family dinner to romantic meals, or simply a business lunch.
When to go	Any day except Sunday. A summer evening for alfresco dining.
Atmosphere	Laid back, friendly and welcoming.
In the know	Parties catered for including privately on Sunday.
Don't just take our word for it	Loyal local clientele, always busy – advisable to book.

Essentials

Run by	The Ventriglia family from Naples.
How big?	60 covers.
Where is it?	Broad Street, tucked away behind town centre. Ample parking nearby.
How much?	From £4.75 for starters, from £9.50 for main courses. Wines from £9.25 – £35.
When is it open?	Lunch and evenings except Sundays.
Get in touch	29a Broad Street Abingdon OX14 3LH ✆ 01235 537676

LOCATION SCOUT: VICTORIA TURNER

Mole Inn Toot Baldon

Gossip & Secrets

The food	An excellent mix of meat and seafood dishes, all served with a twist. Some fantastic flavours and excellent presentation.
The drink	Good wine list including an excellent Chilean Merlot.
Why is it so good?	Landscaped garden is very relaxing to while away the hours in. Inside, the seating is arranged in lots of intimate niches.
Why is it not so good?	Always extremely busy, so spontaneous arrivals may be disappointed.
To die for	Strawberry fool with pistachio praline and strawberry daiquiri.
When to go	Balmy summer evenings are fantastic – but then winter evenings with the open fire are good too!
Atmosphere	Very attentive staff, a lively atmosphere without being too noisy.
Don't just take our word for it	Bib Gourmand in the Michelin Restaurant Guide 2005.

Essentials

Run by	Managed by Chef Patron, Gary Witchalls.
Where is it?	Just off the A4142 Oxford to Wallingford Road.
How much?	Average starter £6, main £12, dessert £6.
When is it open?	Meals served 12pm-2.30pm and 7pm-9.30pm Monday to Saturday. 12pm-9pm on Sundays.
Get in touch	Toot Baldon OX44 9NG ✆ 01865 340001 www.themoleinn.com

LOCATION SCOUT: JILL TRELOGGEN

Country **living**

Fallowfields is a hotel that feels like home – providing home is a 300-year old Cotswold country house. Kick off your shoes and relax.

table was Anthony's grandmother's – even these are somewhat overshadowed by a collection of some 400 elephants acquired as Anthony and Peta travelled India, Asia and Africa in their previous corporate lives.

GREEN FiNGERS

The grounds, complete with panoramic views over the Oxfordshire countryside, are an essential part of Fallowfields, which has two full time gardeners, one who has been with the estate for 27 years. When Anthony and Peta bought the house, they decided to complement the soft, old English focus by planting a full natural vegetable garden, which now supplies the kitchen (and could supply the whole village, it is that big). They also contacted the Brogdale Trust, which holds the National Fruit Collection, to seek advice on planting a mixed British fruit orchard.

Plums, pears and apples bear enough fruit to fulfil demand for home-produced jams, conserves and chutneys used in the kitchen, but also available to buy from reception. Apple pie isn't any old apple pie here; it is a mouth-watering Lanes Prince Albert Apple Pie!

A mooch around the grounds brings further interesting results. How about 19 birds of prey? Fallowfields is home to James Channon and his collection of birds. He trains and demonstrates them at the hotel, and visitors can book lessons or just look on in awe at how well trained these magnificent creatures can become.

THE FRENCH CONNECTiON

Food is a big thing here. Frenchman Charles Leenders is Executive Chef and he strives to create a successful combination of England meets France in his cooking style. He has been with the hotel for five years, and glows with pride when talking about the garden, the produce, and the dishes they create. To fit the needs of his

Weekends in the country are very Bridget Jones. Expectations set sky-high however are often only exceeded by sky-high room charges and the size of your bill on check-out. Moving with a certain 'set' may be fine for some, but it is not for all. Sometimes what you actually want is a home from home – comfortable yet high quality, with service of the highest standards, but discreetly delivered.

Fallowfields was actually bought as a home by Anthony & Peta Lloyd. They then moved into letting rooms, and finally five years ago succumbed to the fickle, demanding yet highly enjoyable trade of being 'mine host' and hotelier. It is a job Anthony, very much the face of Fallowfields, seems cut out for. The hotel feels like home from home – or at least it does if your home is a 300 year old, ten-bedroomed country house in 12 acres of rolling Oxfordshire countryside. Filled with antiques from years of collecting and inheriting – the reception

clients, he does not stick with a compulsory 'restaurant dining experience'. He is not chasing a Michelin star: just aiming to satisfy his customers and provide food that you want to eat, even if it is just a snack.

You can have a light lunch of maybe omelette flavoured with Mrs Montgomery's cheddar on a woodland mushroom sauce (£6.25) on the gorgeous terrace, or a simple sandwich of locally reared and cured ham (£5.50). Lunchtime specials in the restaurant hint at the delights to follow in the evening, and starters might include local game terrine with Fallowfields Champagne rhubarb chutney (£4.75) or fresh garden vegetable soup (£4.50).

Main courses follow a traditional route with difficult choices between Oxfordshire Charolais beef sirloin served with stilton butter (£15.75) or smoked haddock, basil and parmesan mash served with a garden herb cream (£10.75). Puddings are a dream, and might include calvados parfait on crushed amaretto biscuits (£5.25) or traditional crème brulee (£4.25). Dinner time of course moves into more extravagance, and if you cannot be tempted by the eight course gourmet menu priced unbelievably modestly at £59.50, then you will no doubt be lured by Charles' signature dishes of pan fried langoustines and scallops, with fennel marinated in a lime dressing (£10.75), followed by blue Scottish lobster roasted and then flamed in calvados with the claws served in a prawn bisque sauce (approx £37).

If you visit Fallowfields, do not for any reason miss Charles' dessert of warm chocolate surprise with chocolate tagliatelle and avocado and lime ice cream (£6.75). To die for? What a way to go! ∬

ESSENTIALS

Run by Anthony & Peta Lloyd.
How big 10 bedrooms
     Restaurant can seat 35/40
     Lovely Terrace
     Marquee available for special occasions up to
     150 people.
How much Rooms from £150 double inc VAT & breakfast. Special promotions are often run, so phone the hotel for any special offers.
For food costs, see the main article.
Children Very welcome.
Get in touch Fallowfields Country House Hotel
     Faringdon Road
     Kingston Bagpuize
     Oxfordshire
     OX13 5BH
     ✆ 01865 820416
     E stay@fallowfields.com
     www.fallowfields.com

GOSSIP & SECRETS

The food Great for dropping in for lunch or a celebration, they will make you feel welcome whatever the occasion and however much you want to spend!

The drink Aahhh. Anthony is a bit of a connoisseur. He organises gourmet evenings with amazing wines to taste and he is well worth grabbing for a recommendation for dinner.

To die for Charles' Chocolate pudding! Strolling through the orchard and scrumping your own lunch!! (sshh don't tell anyone!)

When to go Anytime. But pre-book for weekends. This hotel is extremely popular with weddings and can get fully booked. Weekday getaways are lovely as the hotel is quieter and you can relax and chill. Enquire about any special offers – they run gourmet mid-week specials as well as cookery lessons and falconry training classes. Winters are fabulous – you have roaring fires and are on the doorstep to the Cotswolds without paying the price!

Atmosphere Chilled-out and unpretentious, a bit like going to stay with good friends. You can curl up with a book in the lounge, or hide in your bedroom and order room service.

The knowledge A small conference room can turn this into an executive retreat very quickly, and Anthony and his team will help make any special event truly memorable.

Don't just take our word for it Oxford has a business networking group that specialises in going to the best places in the county for lunch. Fallowfields has won best restaurant three years on the trot.
Tourism South East – Winner, Small Hotel of the Year 2005. Three RAC Dining Awards.

LOCATION SCOUT Kate Rouse

LOCATION
PARTNER

Hotel du Vin Henley

Gossip & Secrets

The food	French-influenced bistro with daily changing menu. From classics like moules marinieres to great things with fish, chicken and steak.
The drink	Astonishing wine list stretching to over 40 pages. Ask Cyril the sommelier for his recommendations.
Why is it so good?	Chic, stylish, but not pretentious. A real experience.
Why is it not so good?	Smoky if you don't like that sort of thing. The fact there is a cigar room with humidor right next to the bar says it all.
To die for	Stay in the Ruinart, one of three studio suites with an outdoor bath terrace and river views. Drinking champagne at midnight was never this much fun!
Occasions	Romantic nights, lazy weekends, or just dinner if you are local.
When to go	Busy at weekends. More chance of getting a great room and a good table during the week.
Atmosphere	Housed in the old Brakspears Brewery, in keeping with the group's aims: traditional settings with a modern twist.
In the know	Pre-book your parking (done by the valet). The hotel runs a series of great wine tasting events – check the website.
Don't just take our word for it	Best Hotel Group in the UK in the Guardian Travel Awards 2004.

Essentials

Run by	Matt Callard, General Manager
How big?	Hotel – 43 bedrooms. Bistro – 100 covers.
Where is it?	Overlooking the Thames in the centre of Henley.
How much?	Twin/double rooms from £115, studios/suites from £175. Starters £6.75; mains £12.50 to £14.
	Wines – house wines from £13. Then upwards to whatever your wallet can afford. Something for every taste and budget.
When is it open?	Hotel – year round. Last orders: 2pm for lunch, 10pm for dinner.
Get in touch	New Street Henley-on-Thames RG9 2BP. ✆ 01491 848400 www.hotelduvin.com

LOCATION SCOUT: PAUL ROUSE

◄ THE HOTEL DU VIN: DESIGNED FOR DECADENCE.

On Location: Midsomer Murders

The TV series:	Midsomer Murders – ITV (1997 - present)
The locations:	Botanic Garden, High Street, Oxford
	Corn Exchange, Wallingford
	Henley Regatta
	Harpsden Court, Harpsden
	Thame Park, Thame
	The Plough at Great Haseley
	Dorchester-on-Thames (pictured left)
	Little Milton
	Ewelme
	Long Crendon
	Warborough
The stories:	The classic 'murder in an English village' theme updated to the present day. Adapted from the books by Caroline Graham, the series sees Chief Inspector Tom Barnaby (played by John Nettles) pit his wits against eccentric collectors, partner-swapping couples, and a class system in microcosm. Typical Oxfordshire in other words!
The filming:	Filmed mainly in Oxfordshire and Buckinghamshire, Midsomer Murders uses a variety of real-life locations, from Henley Regatta to the Morgan & Associates estate agency in Little Milton, as well as more general backdrops to depict typical English village life.
Did you know?	Harpsden Court was also used in Ultimate Force, starring Ross Kemp, another TV series made by the creators of Midsomer Murders, Bentley Productions.
	Fans of the TV adaptations can buy the book-of-the-series, Midsomer Murders: The Making of An English Crime Classic by Jeff Evans.
Behind the scenes:	Henley Regatta, one of the world's most famous rowing events, takes place every June. ✆ 01491 572153.
	The Botanic Garden in Oxford is open all year round. ✆ 01865 286690.

◄ JOHN NETTLES AS CHIEF INSPECTOR TOM BARNABY ON LOCATION AT THE BOTANIC GARDEN IN OXFORD.

Rofford Manor Little Milton

Essentials

What is it?	House (not open) and two acres of beautiful gardens, which are open to the public through the National Gardens Scheme.
Where is it?	Just off the B480 between Stadhampton and Chalgrove, 10 miles SE of Oxford.
Cost	£3 for the afternoon.
What makes it special?	The gardens give you a sense that they could be achievable in your own garden, lending inspiration to your own planting schemes. Pleached limes, yew hedges and lots of seats tucked away in little arbours surrounded by sweet-smelling flowers.
Best bit?	The vegetable garden, every inch of which is packed (including the walls) with vegetables and trees. An incredible sight, including more fruit trees grown at two feet high which border most of the beds.
Food options	Delicious afternoon teas are available for very reasonable cost. Or take your own picnic.
Got to see/do	The walled gardens surrounding the swimming pool, a stroll down to the more relaxed setting of the rose-covered boat house by the pair of small lakes, or sit in the croquet lawn with its twin herbaceous borders admiring the vista over the ha ha.
In the know	Privately owned by Jeremy Mogford, the gardens supply his restaurants at Gee's, the Old Bank and the Old Parsonage.
	The gardens are only usually open to the public two days a year, although private visits can be arranged for short periods in June and September.
Get in touch	Look up www.ngs.org.uk for opening days, or write to: Rofford Manor, Little Milton, Oxfordshire OX44 7QQ

LOCATION SCOUT: STELLA BOYLES

Truck Festival Steventon

Essentials

What is it?	An annual weekend music festival in July which raises money for Amnesty International and the Mali Development Fund.
Where is it?	Hill Farm at Steventon, near Didcot.
Cost	£27.50 per ticket.
What makes it special?	Truck has evolved over the last seven years but still retains its friendly local atmosphere. Most of the bands are local to the Oxford area, and you always see at least one band you've never heard of whose CD you have go and buy from the tent.
Food options	The local Rotary Club provides burgers, bacon sandwiches, chips, tea, coffee, etc. Vegetarian pasta salads, etc also available.
Got to see/do	Fresh Out The Box at the trailer park tent. Check out the market area and definitely have a banana smoothie.
Get in touch	✆ 01865 722333 www.truckrecords.com

LOCATION SCOUT: SIMON BAKER

World Pooh Sticks Championships Little Wittenham

Essentials

What is it?	An annual event in March, with individuals and teams from all over the world competing to see whose sticks float the fastest along the Thames. Honest!
Where is it?	Days Lock, Little Wittenham, near Dorchester.
What makes it special?	Who hasn't read Winnie The Pooh and played Pooh Sticks? Now you get to do it in serious competition! Great fun for kids.
Best bit?	Winning! Seeing kids' faces light up with delight as they hang over the bridges, willing their sticks to pass the finishing line.
Food options	The local Rotary Club provides burgers, hot dogs, etc. Or bring a picnic (and a warm rug).
Got to see/do	Bouncy castle, face painting and loads of other sideshows.
Get in touch	✆ 01491 838294 www.pooh-sticks.com

LOCATION SCOUT: PAUL ROUSE

Garsington Opera Oxford

Essentials

What is it?
Choice of three opera productions over four weeks in June/July, held on the Garsington Manor terrace with superb acoustics.

Where is it?
Garsington village, just to the East of Oxford.

Cost
£75 upwards, but best to join Friends of Garsington Opera to ensure priority booking. Champagne, picnics and dinner extra, but can bring your own.

What makes it special?
Outdoor opera in beautiful setting – a closer Glyndebourne! Black-tie occasion in superb setting. Marquees available if wet.

Best bit?
Enjoying champagne in the beautiful grounds before the performance and a picnic during the especially long interval.

Food options
Bring your own picnic, or pre-book a hamper. For the really indulgent, pre-book dinner in the Great Barn Restaurant.

Got to see/do
Arrive early to enjoy the extensive grounds and rub shoulders with the occasional royalty and celebrities in the audience.

Get in touch
Garsington Opera Office
✆ 01865 361636
www.garsingtonopera.org

LOCATION SCOUT: STELLA BOYLES

Henley Festival of Music and the Arts

Essentials

What is it?	Eclectic mix of classical, jazz, folk and roots music, theatre, dance, comedy, visual art and family events, including nightly firework spectaculars.
Where is it?	Various venues in the town, including the Floating Stage and the Riverside Lawn.
Cost	Tickets from £23 to £178 depending on events and duration.
What makes it special?	World-class stars such as Kiri Te Kanawa and Vanessa Mae, plus weird and wonderful acts from all sectors of showbiz.
Best bit?	Discovering unknown talent alongside established stars. Fantastic food. And the chance to swan it in style.
Food options	Take your pick — Albert Roux at The Riverside, the Ruinart Champagne Terrace, various bars and restaurants, or corporate hospitality at La Scala.
Got to see/do	Quaff champagne, and listen to great music under the night sky.
Get in touch	✆ 01491 843404.

Henley Regatta

Essentials

What is it?	Annual gathering for the rowing (and hat) brigade. Five days of events in late June/early July.
Where is it?	Where else — down by the river.
Cost	From £10 for a daily ticket. Free if you manage to get invited into the large corporate hospitality section.
What makes it special?	A tradition since 1839, the regatta usually has more to do with the hospitality than the rowing, although those out on the water take it very seriously.
Best bit?	Pimms in the sunshine.
Food options	A variety of bars and restaurants, plus the corporate hospitality tents.
Got to see/do	Usually coincides with Wimbledon — you'll find yourself cheering on the plucky Brits on TV or on the river.
Get in touch	✆ 01491 572153.

LOCATION SCOUT: PAUL ROUSE

A quick guide West Oxfordshire

Where is it?	The gateway to the Cotswolds. Stretching west of Oxford to the Gloucestershire border. Known as the Oxfordshire Cotswolds.
Lifestyle	Market towns, pretty villages and open countryside. Recently voted one of the top ten places to live in the UK.
Main towns	Witney — for pubs.
	Woodstock — for restaurants.
	Burford — for gifts.
	Chipping Norton — for antiques.
Picture postcard views	Bampton, Black Bourton, Shilton, Crawley, Shipton-under-Wychwood, Alvescot, Bladon, Ramsden, Churchill, Minster Lovell.
Historic houses	Blenheim, Chastleton, Kelmscott, Rousham.
Museums	Charlbury, Chipping Norton, Witney, Swinford, Cogges Manor Farm, Oxford Bus Museum, Oxfordshire Museum in Woodstock.
Attractions	Cotswold Wildlife Park, Combe Mill, North Leigh Roman Villa, Rollright Stones, Aston Pottery.
Must do	Take a barge trip along the Thames.
	See the animals at Cotswold Wildlife Park.
	Drive through the ford at Shilton.
	Eat Sicilian couscous at Cafe Messina in Witney.
	Picnic by the lake at Blenheim.
	Shop for antiques in Burford.
Tourist information	Burford ✆ 01993 823590 Witney ✆ 01993 775802 Woodstock ✆ 01993 813276 www.oxfordshirecotswolds.org
In the know	For information on the history, shops and attractions of Woodstock, check out the town's website — www.wakeuptowoodstock.com

◄ WEST OXFORDSHIRE LIFESTYLE: (CLOCKWISE FROM TOP LEFT) BURFORD HOUSE HOTEL; FOXBURY FARM; THE LAMB AT CRAWLEY; WITNEY; THE TROUT AT TADPOLE BRIDGE; BLENHEIM PALACE; COTSWOLD WILDLIFE PARK; WOODSTOCK; BURFORD

The **in-crowd**

The days of wine – and roses – are back at The Fleece in Witney. Eat, drink and celebrate in style.

full-blown three course from an eclectic and ever-changing menu.

Part of Peach Pubs, this privately-owned, independent group is currently winning awards and scooping up local business wherever they open. A young dynamic team of owners combined with excellent local managers and well trained staff shows.

MANY HAPPY RETURNS

I was here to celebrate my birthday. The pub has 10 lovely bedrooms, not super luxurious, but ideal for a group of friends to get together without the hassles of taxis and nominated drivers. In fact, as we took all 10 rooms, we paid only £55 per room per night. And this included a hearty breakfast.

We had booked the private dining room adjacent to the main building, in the courtyard, which held 20 of us nicely. If you have always thought that this kind of 'private dining' arrangement was out of your league, think again. The Fleece specialises in superb and sensibly-priced food that is probably 25-30% cheaper than you would pay at a 'gastro pub.' High quality ingredients, creative menus and of course the now famous Peach Pubs deli board.

We ate, drank, we laughed and we felt like stars. What better way to celebrate any occasion? Even better, there is no room hire charge for a large party. And when we had finished, we trundled upstairs to our rooms ready to take on the world the next day.

GEORGiAN SPLENDOUR

Hangovers are a horrible thing. But a good breakfast and a stiff Bloody Mary later and we were ready for some retail therapy. We took advantage of the westerly location of Witney and shopped until we dropped in Witney, Burford and Bourton-on-the-Water, all within 15 miles of The Fleece.

Remember when your absolute favourite place was a great wine bar? You went there at lunch time with or without clients, and no-one frowned at you for having a bottle of wine or two for lunch. You maybe dropped in after work for a drink, and you went back at weekends with partners and friends because the food was great and the atmosphere relaxed, yet you felt sophisticated and part of the in-crowd.

Well in Witney, those days are back. The Fleece, although technically a pub with bedrooms, has managed to achieve an environment that has the upwardly mobile of West Oxfordshire using it almost as a second home. From breakfast through to the end of the day, the place goes from a gentle buzz to a happy, loud clatter. With a smoking bar at the front and a non-smoking dining area at the back, you can come here for a pint, a coffee, a glass of wine and a quick bite to eat, or a

Witney, on the edge of the Cotswolds, was famed for its blanket making over the centuries, and is a classic market town with a gentle feel to it. The Fleece is situated on The Green, with the most gorgeous (£1 million-plus) Georgian houses sitting around the edge of it, and set off, at the far end, by a beautiful church. On a sunny day, with seats outside, The Fleece and Witney are everything you could ever want from England. Over a glass of wine, we fantasised about who would have lived in the houses in years gone by, who would have been having affairs with whom, and what Jane Austen might have made of it all. I came to the conclusion I would have probably been the scullery maid!

Our weekend was coming to a close, we had eaten and drank (lots!), shopped and laughed and laughed. Our bill was less than £200 per head at The Fleece − not bad for one lunch, one dinner, two breakfasts and two nights stay. Will we be back? Whose birthday is it next? §§

REVIEW: Kate Rouse

CLASSIC
LOCATIONS
FAVOURITE

ESSENTIALS

Run By Hamish Stoddart and John Johnston
How Big Seats 70, with a separate private function room catering for up to 26. They also have 10 rooms for B&B accommodation.
Room Rate £75 per room, but ask for late deals.
How Much Average starter £5, Main £10-12, Dessert £5
Children Fine in the restaurant and outside on The Green. Lots of families eat here at weekends.
Get in touch 11 Church Green
Witney OX28 4AZ
✆ 01993 892270
www.peachpubs.com

GOSSIP & SECRETS

The food Classic dishes are sausage of the week, and risotto of the week. The steaks are excellent, as is the seafood. All-day menu with good selection, plus specials and lunchtime/evening menus, which change regularly.
The drink Not an exhaustive wine list, but some good bottles varying in price from £10-£30.
To die for Location − situated on the Green in Witney, it is an idyllic venue on a sunny day with plenty of seating out the front overlooking the Green. Food wise, try a Charcuterie board − the Piccalilli is 'to die for.'
When to go Very busy every night − booking on a Friday or Saturday is advisable. Half-price champagne night changes − worth checking the website or phoning up!
Atmosphere Lively and friendly atmosphere − with a good mix of clientele − both young and the not so young!
The knowledge Order a coffee − and you get a dish of smarties to go with it. Really comfortable lounge bar at the front which has a good supply of papers, ideal for Sunday breakfast rolling through to lunch!
Don't just take our word for it Voted one of the top 20 pubs in England in 2004 and 2005 by The Morning Advertiser.

LOCATION SCOUT Jill Treloggen

LOCATION
PARTNER

Hand & Shears Church Hanborough

Gossip & Secrets

The food	Freshly cooked British Cuisine with a Mediterranean twist. Hugely comprehensive menu, from light lunchtime bites to full a la carte dining by candlelight. Wonderfully inventive fish dishes, excellent vegetarian choices, home made pasta, etc.
The drink	Interesting wine list with an excellent choice of bin ends.
Why is it so good?	A young family-run business whose aim is to please.
Why is it not so good?	No garden, only a small outside area to the front on the road.
To die for	Fillet of Sea Bass served on a bed of samphire grass with citrus butter and pink peppercorn sauce or Pork Loin Steak, stuffed with Black Pudding and Sausage meat with Apricot Compote.
Occasions	Romantic dinner for two, or Sunday Lunch with the family.
When to go	Live jazz Friday nights and Sunday lunchtimes.
Atmosphere	Has the look and feel of a town restaurant but in a country village setting. Contemporary art adorns the walls, giving local artists a realistic opportunity to exhibit and sell their work. Leading down several steps from the small cosy bar area, in to the large and airy restaurant, it is softly lit, making it feel quite intimate.
In the know	Live music and cocktail jazz on Friday nights, and Lounge Jazz Sunday lunch times (subject to change – please phone to check beforehand). For parties of eight, ask for the large round table in the raised section of the restaurant.

Essentials

How big?	70 covers.
Where is it?	In the small village of Church Hanborough just off the A40, between Witney and Woodstock. Parking in car park opposite.
How much?	Starters £5, mains £11.95; desserts £3.95.
When is it open?	Closed all day Monday. Open Tuesday to Sunday, 11.30am-3pm and 6.00pm-11.00pm.
Get in touch	Church Hanborough OX28 8AB ✆ 01993 883337

LOCATION SCOUT: ALISON PETRASH

The Lamb Crawley

Gossip & Secrets

The food	Traditional English, fabulous selection. You must try the half shoulder of lamb.
The drink	Reasonably priced – bottle of house wine £14.
Why is it so good?	Friendly service, good food with generous portions, but presented as a top restaurant would.
Why is it not so good?	You often have to book well in advance.
To die for	Stilton mushrooms are a must – they melt in your mouth.
Occasions	Anytime, whether it is a meal for 2 or 12. They also have a private room that you can book for parties.
When to go	Saturday nights are very busy and you would not get a table on spec. Lunchtimes are fairly busy.
Atmosphere	Relaxed atmosphere. Children are very welcome and families often gather for Sunday lunch.
In the know	Book well in advance if you are a party of 10+ – ask for the side room.

Essentials

Run by	Andy Dearie.
How big?	Would seat 70 people between the various rooms and also approx. 20 more on the terrace.
Where is it?	On the main road into the quaint village of Crawley, near Witney.
How much?	Average starter £5, main course £10-£15, dessert £4.
Get in touch	Leafield Road Crawley OX29 9TW Ø 01993 703753

LOCATION SCOUT: CLAIRE WILLCOX

Golden Pheasant Burford

Gossip & Secrets

The food	Good, old-fashioned English pub fare – steak & kidney pie, beer-battered cod and pan-fried venison among many others.
The drink	Greene King, Old Speckled Hen and a wide choice of wines.
Why is it so good?	Manages to combine the best of being a hotel, pub and restaurant without compromising. Comfortable and comforting. Hasn't fallen into the tourist trap despite its position and popularity.
Why is it not so good?	Parking in Burford can be a nightmare – and it's right on the High Street.
Occasions	Rest those weary shopping feet at weekends, or drop in during the week for a quieter meal.
Atmosphere	Busy bar for the locals, two separate but integrated restaurant spaces for diners.
In the know	Excellent live music on Friday nights from local bands. Also has ten bedrooms.

Essentials

Run by	Martin Lyall
How big?	Tardis-like inside, belying its coaching inn frontage.
Where is it?	Halfway down Burford's famous hill, on the right hand side.
How much?	Two-course meal from around £15-£20. Rooms – £95 for a four-poster.
When is it open?	Restaurant serves lunch from 12-2pm and dinner from 6.30-9pm. Normal pub hours for drinkers.
Get in touch	High Street Burford OX18 4QA ☏ 01993 823223.

LOCATION SCOUT: PAUL ROUSE

Burford House Burford

Gossip & Secrets

The food	'Hard to decide' light lunch menu. Grilled Somerset Capricorn Goats Cheese with toasted pine nuts and mixed leaves, Smoked Duck Salad and daily specials – mouth-watering stuff!
The drink	Cosy help-yourself bar. Homemade Sloe Gin plus a good selection of malts and brandies.
Why is it so good?	Very relaxed, excellent old world service, spotlessly clean and unpretentious. Great sandwiches and homemade cakes.
Why is it not so good?	No evening meals – lunchtime light meals only. No car park.
To die for	Homemade fruit tart – their speciality. Potted shrimps from Morecambe Bay.
When to go	Special breaks available – ring to check.
Atmosphere	Traditional coffee shop/tearoom atmosphere. Friendly helpful staff. 17th century building, oak beams, etc.
In the know	Try the sun-trap patio garden. Book the Sherbourne suite with Venetian marble tiling and roll top bath.
Don't just take our word for it	English Tourism Council Gold Award. AA 5 Diamonds.

Essentials

Run by	Simon and Jan Henty
How big?	8 rooms (plus two lounges, Honour Bar).
Where is it?	Right in the middle of the town on the corner of the High Street and Witney Street.
How much?	Ranging from £125 – £155 per night (single occupancy ranging from £90). All have Sky TV.
When is it open?	All year round.
Get in touch	99 High Street Burford OX18 4QA ✆ 01993 823151

LOCATION SCOUT: BRIAN SINFIELD

Tite Inn Chadlington

Gossip & Secrets

The food	Good pub food. English home cooking – brilliant fillet and rib-eye steak and homemade puddings.
The drink	Real beer pub – five draught beers, one draught cider and a comprehensive wine list.
Why is it so good?	This is one of those rare old-time country locals – no fruit machines or loud music in this one. Mike, the owner, is seldom away from the bar and has an opinion on everything, which results in some interesting discussions. Everyone welcome including children and dogs, but leave muddy boots outside!
Why is it not so good?	Closed Mondays (except Bank Holiday lunch times)
Occasions	Easter Egg Rolling Championship held every Easter Monday – very popular. Annual Pantomime – hilarious. Winter Weekly Specials on Wednesdays – extraordinarily good value.
Atmosphere	Relaxed, unpretentious – no frills. This is a friendly local pub that does food. Roaring log fire in the winter and interesting people to meet.
In the know	Separate dining if you want privacy or eat in the bar and soak up atmosphere. The pub is a favourite with local MP David Cameron.
Don't just take our word for it	AA Good Pub Guide; CAMRA Good Pub Guide; WHICH Country Pub Guide – Winner of North Oxfordshire Pub of the Year 2005.

Essentials

Run by	Owned and run for the past 16 years by Mike and Sue Willis.
How big?	60 covers plus additional eating outside in summer.
Where is it?	Chadlington village (bottom end) 1 mile approx off A361 Chipping Norton – Shipton under Wychwood road.
How much?	Average Starter – £4.95 Average main – £9.00 Average Pudding – £3.95
When is it open?	Tues–Sat 12 – 2.30 pm and 6.30 (7.00 on Sundays) – 11.00 pm
Get in touch	Mill End Chadlington OX7 3NY ✆ 01608 676475 www.titeinn.com

LOCATION SCOUT: BRIAN SINFIELD

Chequers Churchill

Gossip & Secrets

The food	Traditional meets modern: superb roast beef and Yorkshire pudding, but also breast of guinea fowl, pan-fried marlin steak, goats cheese & roasted bell pepper strudel, and grilled seabass fillet.
The drink	Hook Norton plus guest beers, and a good wine list.
Why is it so good?	Modern transformation of an 18th century Cotswold village pub without losing the character. Spacious and light separate dining area at the back does not interfere with the pub at the front. The lovely Irish landlady, Assumpta, has a warm welcome for everybody.
Why is it not so good?	Almost too popular at times – you will need to book for Sunday lunch in particular.
Occasions	Early Sunday lunch before the real crowds appear, or any evening.
Atmosphere	Bustling bar, full of locals and walkers. Restaurant ideal for families: boisterous kids get drowned out anyway by the hubbub!
In the know	The quieter section upstairs is easily missed.

Essentials

Size	The restaurant extension makes it deceptively spacious.
Where is it?	Off the Burford to Chipping Norton road (A361), opposite the village church.
How much?	Two-course meal from around £15-£20.
When is it open?	Restaurant serves lunch from 12-2pm (3pm on Sundays) and dinner from 7-9.30pm (9pm on Sundays). Normal pub hours for drinkers.
Get in touch	Church Road Churchill OX7 6NJ ∅ 01608 659393.

LOCATION SCOUT: PAUL ROUSE

The Vines Black Bourton

Gossip & Secrets

The food	Eclectic: Mediterranean but with English, Middle East and Thai dishes available.
The drink	Good beer selection, as it is primarily a pub. Over 30 wines, including some from Oxfordshire vineyards.
Why is it so good?	You don't expect such a sophisticated menu in a quiet country pub.
Why is it not so good?	Well off the beaten track. Diners sometimes get odd looks from the yokel (sorry, local) drinkers.
When to go	Leisurely business lunch. Special event nights.
Atmosphere	Cool, calm, collected in the restaurant. Down to earth in the bar.
In the know	The Mediterranean-style restaurant was designed by the BBC Real Rooms makeover programme. Runs regular jazz evenings and Egyptian Nights: co-owner Ahdy is from Cairo.

Essentials

Run by	Karen and Ahdy Gerges.
How big?	Relatively small dining area. Best to book.
Where is it?	Quiet village between Bampton and Alvescot. Easy to miss – check website for directions.
How much?	Starters £3.95-£6.95; mains £10.45-£15.50; desserts £4.25.
When is it open?	Lunchtimes and evenings. A la carte menu served Mon-Sat. Traditional roast on Sundays.
Get in touch	Burford Road Black Bourton Nr Bampton OX18 2PF ✆ 01993 843559 www.vinesblackbourton.co.uk

LOCATION SCOUT: PAUL ROUSE

The Trout Tadpole Bridge

Gossip & Secrets

The food	Owner and chef Chris Green has a passion for fresh local ingredients. Small but interesting menu supported by a daily specials board with a good choice of fish and meat. Despite winning a number of food awards, you can also drop in for a sandwich.
The drink	Great wine list with over 10 by the glass. They do not sell half bottles, but will open any bottle under £25 and only charge you for what you have consumed. Good beers and guest ales.
Why is it so good?	Traditional 17th century pub with a fabulous location on the banks of the Thames. The Thames path runs on the opposite side of the river, and is great for a gentle walk. Large beer garden. Worth booking a table, as it gets very busy.
Why is it not so good?	The staff behind the bar can be a bit frosty. Popular place for locals and occasionally has a bit of an 'in-crowd' feel to it.
To die for	A standard of food you would not expect from such a down-to-earth pub. They have not sold out to the pub-diner mentality.
Occasions	Great for lunch after a good walk, nice for a family celebration, and as dogs and children are all welcome, combine the two.
When to go	Summer is lovely as the gardens back onto the Thames. But winter sees log fires and really cosy afternoons with the papers.
In the know	A private function room can be booked for a party of 40, or used for corporate meetings. Plus six lovely bedrooms.
Don't just take our word for it	Good Pub Guide – Oxfordshire Dining Pub of the Year 2005.

Essentials

How big?	Three sections to the main dining area seating 60, plus the private room seating 40. Outside seating for 100+
Where is it?	Down a country lane off the A420, signposted for Bampton.
How much?	Starters from £5.95, mains from £8.95 to £14.95.
When is it open?	Closed 3pm – 5.30pm. Also check Christmas and New Year.
Get in touch	Tadpole Bridge Buckland Marsh Faringdon SN7 8RF ✆ 01367 870382 www.trout-inn.co.uk

LOCATION SCOUT: KATE ROUSE

A traditional Oxfordshire Breakfast

To Drink

Apple Juice	Bensons Fruit Juices, Sherborne, Oxfordshire. ✆ 01451 844134	Sold at pubs, restaurants, delis, farm shops & farmers' markets, including Deddington.
Pear Juice	Q-Gardens Farm Shop & PYO, Abingdon, Oxfordshire. ✆ 01235 820988	Found at their own farm shop and other local farm shops, delis and farmers' markets, including Deddington.

To Start

Muesli	Sally's Muesli of Bampton, Oxfordshire. ✆ 01993 850479	Sold at Foxbury Farm Shop and various other outlets.
Natural Yogurt	Tim's Dairy, Gerrards Cross, Bucks. ✆ 01753 888380	Found at Local Tastes in Thame.
Fresh Fruit	Highclose Farm Shop and PYO, Hungerford, Berks. ✆ 01488 686770	Sold at their own farm shop and farmers' markets outside of Oxfordshire, including Reading.

Tucking In

Sausage	Foxbury Farm Shop & Butchery, Brize Norton, Oxfordshire. ✆ 01993 844141	Found at their own farm shop, farmers' markets including Stow and Tackley, and Ascot Village Shops.
Bacon	Dews Meadow Farm, Wantage, Oxfordshire. ✆ 01235 868634	Sold at their own farm shop, farmers' markets including Abingdon, and local stores.
Eggs	Barrington Organic Eggs, Burford, Oxfordshire. ✆ 01451 844306	Found at numerous local farm shops and stores.
Tomatoes	Grove Farm PYO, Leighton Buzzard, Beds. ✆ 01296 668834	Visit the farm shop and PYO and pick your very own tomatoes for breakfast.
Fried Bread/ Toast	Bread and Co, Banbury, Oxfordshire. ✆ 01295 758489	Stalls at various town and farmers' markets, including Banbury.

Side Orders

Mustard	Shaken Oak Products, Witney, Oxfordshire. ✆ 01993 355969	In farm shops including Foxbury Farm Shop, delis and local stores.
Marmalade	Quince Products, Aston Rowant, Oxfordshire. ✆ 01491 614664	Found at Local Tastes in Thame, The Granary at Watlington, Henley Farmers' Market or via mail order.

Shaken Oak Products Witney

What do they produce?	Range of mustards, sauces and dressings.
What makes them special?	Only the finest ingredients are used and where possible sourced locally. No additives.
Behind the scenes	Shaken Oak mustard making started as a hobby to please friends and family.
How much?	Prices vary from £1.95 to £4.00.
In the know	Products are made in small batches and only traditional methods of manufacture are used.
To die for	Old Hooky Beer Mustard - delicious with all meat, vegetables and cheese dishes.
Where can I get them?	Foxbury Farm Shop in Brize Norton, Local Tastes in Thame and Mrs Bumbles in Burford.
Get in touch	Old North Leigh Lane Hailey Witney OX29 9UX ✆ 01993 868043 www.shakenoak.co.uk

LOCATION SCOUT: PAUL ROUSE

Star-**studded**

The Bear is ideal for romantic breaks – and the rich and famous obviously agree.

The Bear Hotel
Park Street
Woodstock OX20 1SZ
0870 400 8202
bear@macdonald-hotels.co.uk
www.bearhotelwoodstock.co.uk

Part of my fondness for The Bear lies in the company you enjoy at dinner. Two fabulous teddy bears, each the size of a small child, sit in the restaurant, and go by the rather grand names of William and Winston. It sets the scene for this lovely hotel, rich in history, with an inn present here since 1279.

The Bear today however is firmly planted in the 21st century, mixing romance, escape and great food with the glorious past of Woodstock and neighbouring Blenheim Palace.

The 54 bedrooms offer wireless broadband and CDs alongside the comfort and luxury you would expect from one of Britain's most famous hotels. Perhaps its most celebrated guests were Elizabeth Taylor and Richard Burton at the height of their romance, and the Marlborough Suite even has pillows embroidered with E and R in memory of those halcyon days. More recently, guests have included Mick Jagger, John Malkovich and Johnny Depp.

FOCAL POINT

The picture-postcard town of Woodstock is a focal point for this delightful corner of Oxfordshire, sitting so close to the Cotswolds that it frequently gets claimed by both tourism areas. Streets lined with charming shops selling antiques, home interiors and exclusive fashions sit happily alongside a great selection of pubs and restaurants. Woodstock of course also boasts one of England's most treasured houses, Blenheim Palace, which is walking distance from The Bear and makes the hotel a popular choice for festival and concert-goers.

The Bear has two AA Rosettes for its food, and combines a modern European approach with a touch of fusion flair: a seasonally changing menu allows for the sampling of new ideas, from asparagus mousse with truffle creme fraiche and tomato jelly to tortellini of crab with baby spinach and cappuccino of bisque. A 12-page wine list with an extensive list of wines by the glass just adds to the challenge, but these are the type of choices to relish. ♫

ESSENTIALS

Run by Gaius Wyncoll, General Manager. Part of Macdonald Hotels.

How big 54 bedrooms. Restaurant can seat 80.

A selection of private rooms, some housed in the old Woodstock Glove Factory, can be used for conferences or private dining.

Exclusive use of both hotel and restaurants can be arranged for weddings or parties.

How much Look on the website for up-to-date room rates as they change season to season.

Table d'hote menu: Lunch – £20.95. Dinner – £25.95 for three courses. Sunday lunch – £24.95. A la carte: average starter – £7, main course – £22, dessert – £6

Children Will love it!

Get in touch The Bear Hotel

Park Street

Woodstock OX20 1SZ

☏ 0870 400 8202

bear@macdonald-hotels.co.uk

www.bearhotelwoodstock.co.uk

GOSSIP & SECRETS

The food Excellent modern European. The chef does lunch demonstrations that take place monthly, and involve eating a four-course lunch that he has cooked in front of your eyes.

The drink Excellent wine list and a traditional coaching inn bar that serves good light food options as well.

To die for Teddies at the restaurant table or a four poster bed – can't decide which!

When to go Anytime you want to spoil or treat someone.

Atmosphere Clandestine meetings, affairs and romance.

The knowledge Woodstock is a fabulous place to stay for a two or three day break. Great shops, Blenheim Palace and plenty of nearby places to explore, including Oxford.

Don't just take our word for it AA 3-star hotel. Two AA Rosettes for the food.

LOCATION SCOUT: Kate Rouse

Foxbury Farm Shop Brize Norton

Local products	Foxbury Farm beef, lamb and Gloucester Old Spot pork, Shaken Oak mustard, Abbeygold cheese, Matthews flour, Upper Norton jersey cream, Bensons fruit juices, Oxford cheese.
Further afield	Bennetts ice cream from Worcestershire, Tyrrells crisps from Herefordshire, Godminster cheese from Somerset.
What makes them special?	One of the few genuine farm shops in the area, the lamb, beef and pork come from animals reared on the farm, offering full traceability. Fruit and veg is from local farms, and all produce is seasonal. Worth the drive for asparagus and broad beans in the summer.
Behind the scenes	Foxbury is a family business, and you will find Colin, Di, Rebecca and Stuart working in the shop and the farm.
How much?	Rib of beef – £7.48 per kg Whole leg of lamb – £8.48 per kg The Old Spot Banger Sausage – £5.85 per kg
In the know	Make friends with John the butcher and his team – the banter always makes a visit here entertaining. They also make a variety of speciality products like the St George's Day Dragon Burger and the love sausage for Valentine's Day. They will cut meat to order, however complicated that new recipe from Jamie or Nigella may be.
	Foxbury also offer a delivery service in a 30 mile radius.
To die for	The range of Foxbury Fast Feast Ready Made Meals and home-cooked produce, with no additives, preservatives or colourings in use. Also try their Moroccan Lamb.
Don't just take our word for it	National Meat Producer of the Year 2002
	South East England Excellence in Meat Products Awards 2002/2003.
	England's Top Farm Shop – Meat Trades Journal Awards 2005
	Cotswold Life Best Farm Shop 2005
Get in touch	Foxbury Farm Shop Brize Norton OX18 3NX ✆ 01993 844141 www.foxburyfarm.co.uk

LOCATION SCOUT: KATE ROUSE

Aston Pottery Aston

Essentials

What is it?	Working pottery, gift & coffee shop.
Where is it?	Slightly off the beaten track in Aston, just beyond Bampton, near to Witney. Pretty drive, and well worth the effort.
Cost	Only tours of the pottery and special events carry a small charge.
What makes it special?	Truly a "feel-good" experience. Something for everyone including toys to amuse the children while you indulge in cake and coffee. Delightful staff and original gifts to choose from, and also to treat yourself to. It's impossible to leave empty handed.
Best bit?	The unique hand-stencilled pottery which can also be personalised.
Got to see/do	The full pottery tour.
Get in touch	The Stable Kingsway Farm Aston OX18 2BT ✆ 01993 851877 www.astonpottery.co.uk

LOCATION SCOUT: TRACEY JEFFERIES

Manfred Schotten Antiques Burford

Essentials

Style	Fabulous display set in 15th century building. Amazing features and ancient crypt.
Size	Large — four showrooms and full of a huge range of fascinating and rare sporting antiques: billiard tables, pictures, ceramics — anything relating to sport and games. This is one of the leading shops of its kind in Britain.
Cost	From a huge range of small items suitable for gifts up to seriously priced collectors' pieces — virtually something for everyone of a sporting mind.
Exclusive stockists of:	Particularly strong in items relating to golf, fishing, tennis, cricket, polo and rowing.
Get in touch	109 High Street Burford OX18 4RG ✆ 01993 822302 www.schotten.com

LOCATION SCOUT: BRIAN SINFIELD

Cotswold Woollen Weavers Filkins

Essentials

Style	Traditional with contemporary twist. Distinctive and desirable textiles woven on site — clothing, accessories, luxurious rugs, cushions and throws.
Size	Working woollen mill using Victorian looms housed in splendid 18th century Cotswold barns — industrial revolution stuff. Showrooms, museum, coffee shop, plenty of parking.
Cost	Considering their cloth is used by some of the best fashion houses, excellent value! The owners, Richard and Jane Martin, have built this business from scratch over a number of years.
Exclusive stockists of:	You can only buy these unique products here.
Where is it?	Just in Oxfordshire, on the Gloucestershire borders, 5 miles south of Burford.
Get in touch	Filkins near Lechlade GL7 3JJ ⌀ 01367 860491 www.naturalbest.co.uk

LOCATION SCOUT: BRIAN SINFIELD

Blenheim Palace Woodstock

Gossip & Secrets

What is it?	One of England's most famous stately homes. Built by Vanbrugh in the early 18th century and still going strong. Ancestral home of the Dukes of Marlborough and the birthplace of Winston Churchill.
Where is it?	In the village of Woodstock, eight miles north of Oxford.
Cost	See opposite for normal entry prices. Ticket prices vary for special events.
What makes it special?	Steeped in history. Impressive architecture and attractive gardens (but don't expect Versailles). Fabulous lake. Puts on a wide range of events to suit a wide range of interests, from craft fairs and history exhibitions to air displays and concerts.
Downside	Prices can be a bit steep for some events.
Best bit?	Depends of course on your tastes. For me, the Festival of Flight was stupendous – a great day of exhilarating air displays (including the Red Arrows), nostalgia and entertainment. Kids will also love the maze.
Food options	The Garden Café or the Terrace Café for snacks, or the Terrace Restaurant for table d'hote menu or full afternoon tea. Or take your own picnic and sit in the grounds.
Got to see/do	The maze. The Churchill Exhibition.
Get in touch	Blenheim Palace Woodstock OX20 1PX ✆ 08700 602080 www.blenheimpalace.com

LOCATION SCOUT: PAUL ROUSE

On Location: Oxfordshire in the movies

The backdrop:	Oxfordshire's stately homes have featured in a host of (mainly) historic movies.
The famous ones:	Broughton Castle near Banbury was used in The Madness of King George (1994) and Shakespeare In Love (1998), as well as Three Men and a Little Lady (1990) – not a costume drama, unless you include Tom Selleck's checked shirts.
	Edgcote Hall near Banbury featured in the 1995 TV adaptation of Pride and Prejudice starring Colin Firth.
Starring role:	Blenheim Palace at Woodstock has starred in numerous films, including Greystoke (1984), Indiana Jones and the Last Crusade (1989), Kenneth Branagh's Hamlet (1996), The Four Feathers (2002) and The Libertine (2005) starring Johnny Depp.
	The birthplace of Winston Churchill, Blenheim naturally featured in the 1972 biopic Young Winston, starring Simon Ward.
	Blenheim was also used in Entrapment, the 1999 thriller starring Sean Connery and Catherine Zeta Jones.
Not a lot of people know that:	Best forgotten, perhaps, is Blenheim's role in the 1973 low-budget horror movie The Legend of Hell House.
Behind the scenes:	Blenheim Palace is open from February to October, with restricted winter opening times in November and December. Admission: £13 (house and gardens), £8 (gardens only). Concessions and group rates available.

▼ FILMING THE LIBERTINE (2005) AT BLENHEIM PALACE

Cogges Manor Farm Museum Witney

Essentials

What is it?	A working farm museum about life in Victorian times, although some bits of the farm go back even further in history. Has live farm animals, old-fashioned machinery, and carts.
Where is it?	Cogges area of Witney, walking distance from Waitrose.
Cost	Adult day ticket – £4.40. Adult season ticket – £26.00. Children (3–16) day ticket – £2.30. Children season ticket – £14.00. Family (2 adults, 2 children) – £12.90. Family season ticket – £77.00. Concessions – £2.85. Concessions season ticket – £17.00.
What makes it special?	Hand-milking the cows, feeding the pigs and watching butter being made. They have themed weekends throughout the season – which is from Easter time until end of October. And they also have an advent weekend in December. I have done special activities over the holidays from when I was old enough until now. I have made corn dollies, peg dolls, fed the lambs and learnt about farm life in Victorian days.
Best bit?	The animals, because you get to meet them and see them being fed. We also like strolling around by the Windrush River. I also got an old English Rabbit from there and we called him "Cogges."
Food options	Cafe on site of old cow shed. Snacks, home made cakes, drinks, ice creams and some main meals. Can also buy eggs from the farm.
Got to see/do	Victorian maids and manor house, like it would have looked like in Victorian age. Also looking at the animals and being involved with them (I sponsored a Tamworth pig called Marmalade for three years) and then sponsored the donkey, Mattie. Walks around the woods and orchard. And my Mum loves the walled kitchen garden.
When is it open?	Easter to late October. Times vary. Check website.
Get in touch	Church Lane Witney OX28 3LA ✆ 01993 772602 www.cogges.org

LOCATION SCOUT: LEAH EVERTON (AGE 10)

Cotswold Wildlife Park Burford

Essentials

What is it?
Exciting wildlife park with unusual and varied species of animals. With lots of fun things to do too. My mum likes the gardens.

Where is it?
On the A361.

Cost
Adults – £8.50.
Children – £6.00.
Senior Citizens – £6.00.
Under 3's – free.

What makes it special?
As well as lots of animals like Egyptian fruit bats, it even has a train and a children's playground!

Best bit?
Watching the rare Amur Leopards at feeding time. It was fascinating – and scary – to get so close to them.

Food options
Sandwiches, chips, fish cakes, jacket potatoes, hot and cold drinks, ice creams.

Got to see/do
Must go on the train, watch the fruit bats, go to the reptile house, see the leopards, and see the insect house – especially the huge tarantulas!

Get in touch
Cotswold Wildlife Park and Gardens Burford OX18 4JW
☏ 01993 823006
www.cotswoldwildlifepark.co.uk

LOCATION SCOUT: ALEX DOLPHIN (AGE 8)

Location Scouts

All the reviews in this book are independently written, with the benefit of informed local knowledge, by our Location Scouts: professional people who live and work in Oxfordshire. Our thanks to them for their contributions.

SIMON BAKER

Simon is the Gallery Manager of the Marmalade Café & Gallery in Oxford, a venture he co-founded in 2005. Its main focus is on providing fresh, organic and affordable food, but the gallery also aims to provide a space for local, contemporary artists to exhibit and sell their work.

Simon started out as a screen printer and moved on to become a digital printer and pre-press technician. From there, he went on to work as a web developer before moving to the visual arts publisher Purple House, where he worked on a range of publications and websites, and helped develop the weekly on-line magazine, Creativebase News Wires.

When he left Purple House in 2001, he started his own interactive and graphic design company, Media Escape, who are still going strong today.

GORDON BEACH

Gordon has worked in the banking industry for more than 30 years, with most of his career spent with HSBC Bank in a wide variety of roles, before leaving to set up his own consultancy business. He now assists companies in obtaining a wide range of banking services.

A past President of the Chartered Institute of Bankers in Oxfordshire, he has always had a keen interest in business and education links, having served on the Oxford City Education Business Partnership and acted as past Chairman of the Oxfordshire Young Enterprise Board, where he is still actively involved. Currently, he also serves on the fundraising committee for the Oxford Children's Hospital, is Chairman of Eynsham Parish Council, and a Trustee and Director for One City Oxford.

Married with two teenage children, Gordon and his wife Diane have lived in Eynsham for 16 years. They enjoy eating out, the theatre and holidays, mainly in France and Italy.

ALAN BERMAN

Alan is a Director of Berman Guedes Stretton Architects in Oxford. Having moved his architectural practice from London to Oxford in 1987, he now works for a wide range of clients, including Oxford Colleges. He makes hand-built ceramics in Oxford and the south of France, where he spends as much time as possible with his sculptor wife and two daughters.

Aiming to create opportunities for artists in an environment where the visual arts get scant support compared to literature and music, Alan is Chair of Oxford's Artweeks Festival, helped create the OVADA Gallery, of which he is a board member, and is a board member of Oxford Inspires, Oxford's cultural development agency. While holidaying in Italy, Alan also initiated a residency programme for artists to work on a Tuscan estate, now funded by Arts Council Southeast.

Pleasures and pastimes: looking at paintings, time spent barefoot reading alone, or dining with friends under blue skies. Failing in his deepest ambition to play the piano (substituting for this a mastery of the CD player), Alan derives constant satisfaction when managing to persuade bureaucrats and corporates to break their own rules — to which end his South African background is immensely useful.

STELLA BOYLES

After 25 years in motorsport, as both organiser and competitor, and the last 10 years working for Peugeot in Coventry, Stella had a complete career change in 2004 after being frustrated with finding property in Oxfordshire.

She took the opportunity to set up Property One Stop, a glossy magazine which displays homes in price and location order, plus related features to make this publication a must when looking for Oxfordshire property. Having been interested in property for many years with a small portfolio of her own, she has ensured that the magazine meets the needs of the searcher, as well as the vendor and landlord.

Now based in Bloxham near Banbury, the company has become well known for being a useful tool in the search for property through its powerful website and e-newsletter as well as the colourful magazine.

Stella originally hails from Aberdeenshire and returns as often as she can, but when trips allow in Oxfordshire, she likes to relax by wandering round peaceful gardens. "I'm always cooking and enjoy seeing productive vegetable gardens, as well as ones which are beautiful on the eye. Quite a contrast from fast cars."

KIRSTY BRACKENRIDGE

Kirsty joined Modern Art Oxford as Head of Marketing and Development in November 2003, after working in London for nearly ten years, at Event, a design company that specialises in exhibitions and visitor attractions, and previously as a book editor. She graduated in 1994 with a first class honours degree in English and American Literature from Manchester University. Kirsty is married and lives in Oxford.

JANINE CHARLES

Janine is Development Director for OVADA, a new visual arts development agency for Oxfordshire which she helped to found in 2004. Her recent background is in teaching in Higher Education, arts consultancy and arts management.

MICHAEL COCKMAN

Michael first became fascinated by the hotel industry while working at British Airways, where he looked after the company's international hotel investments. He was persuaded to leave the airline industry and took over the marketing activity for a large hotel in London before being lured to New Zealand with the promise of an area that included Fiji and Tahiti!

On returning to the UK, he became Marketing Director for a hotel and pub company, successfully launching the Rainforest Cafe in London's Shaftesbury Avenue plus the Waxy O'Connor's group of Irish pubs.

Michael now runs his own Oxford-based consultancy, The Hotel Coach, working with owners and managers of independent hotels, coaching them to develop the organisation and their skills, to maximise room revenue. He has also been commissioned to write a book on the subject of marketing for independent hotels. In his spare time, he tries to spend as much time as he can with his grandchildren, and do what he can to promote the benefits of the Oxfordshire region.

REBECCA DAWES

On work experience with Classic Locations during the entire publishing process, Rebecca is currently an 'A' level student at Cirencester College, and is planning to go to university in 2006 to study event management and journalism. She lives in West Oxfordshire, and enjoys being part of the success of her parents' award-winning farm shop. She describes herself as "a very determined character who strives to succeed in everything that she does," and her ultimate ambition is to run her own events management company. We have no doubt she will succeed!

MIKE DENNIS

Mike is Head of Public Programmes at The Oxford Trust, which exists to encourage the study, application and communication of science technology and engineering.

Originally a primary school teacher in Oxfordshire before managing The Trust's original hands-on science centre, Curioxity, he has developed a number of science shows and workshops for schools, and has been involved in The Oxfordshire Science Festival since it began in 1992. He set up The Oxfordshire Family Science Programme which graduated to become The Oxfordshire Science Programme.

Educated at Preston and Oxford Polytechnics, he has lived in Oxfordshire since completing his PGCE. He is married with three boys and lives in Headington, near the famous shark. He likes theatre, books and sport, especially Plymouth Argyle.

TED DEWAN

Ted has been an illustrator and cartoonist since 1988. He studied engineering, electronic music and art (with David Macaulay) at Brown University in Rhode Island, and then taught high-school physics for five years in Boston. He now lives in Oxford with his wife, author/illustrator Helen Cooper, and their daughter, Pandora.

Moving to Oxford allowed him to work closely with David Fickling at David Fickling Books, a short bike ride from his home. Author Philip Pullman gave him his famous shed in 2002, so long as he did creative work in it and promised to pass it on to another artist, writer, or musician when he was finished with it, if it hadn't turned to dust in the meantime. The shed was duly blessed in a ceremony in 2003 which nearly set the shed on fire.

After becoming a father in 1998, he decided to dedicate most of his time to writing and illustrating books. He also reviews books and illustrates for The Times Educational Supplement and is a former chairman of the Children's Writers and Illustrators Group (CWIG) of the Society of Authors.

MICHELLE DICKSON

Currently Deputy Director (Programme) at The Oxford Playhouse, Michelle has been working in theatre for nine years, five of which have been spent at Oxford Playhouse. On graduating from Oxford University, she began at the Playhouse in a variety of roles, including working backstage, in marketing, and as the Directors' Assistant. She returned to Oxford three years ago, having worked at the British Council, developing and promoting British drama and dance to theatres and festivals in Western Europe and Africa, and at Ambassador Theatre Group, a commercial theatre company, where she worked on the programming of seven regional theatres.

In her current role, Michelle is responsible for the day-to-day programming of the Playhouse, which involves seeing lots of theatre, dance, music and comedy, looking after home-grown productions, and managing a busy team.

HELEN GANLY

Helen was born in Cookham, Berkshire in 1940. She studied at the Slade School of Fine Art in London from 1958 to 1962 before moving to Oxford, where she taught at The Ruskin School of Drawing and Fine Art, and later in the Education Department of Oxford Brookes University. In 2000, she was given an Artist Award to be the first Artist In Residence at the Ashmolean Museum in Oxford. She is currently working on a forthcoming exhibition in Poland.

BERNARD GOODCHILD

Bernard enjoyed a long career in banking and finance with a major UK clearing bank, and has lived locally since the early 1990s, when he was appointed to take on the general management responsibilities for the bank's branches in Oxfordshire. On the road to senior management, Bernard and his wife Julie found themselves moving house some 11 times during their first 20 years of marriage. They have been particularly pleased therefore to live in the delightful surroundings of North Oxfordshire for the past 12 years.

Since leaving banking in 1998, Bernard has been providing business advisory support to local businesses as an independent consultant, and via his role for Oxford Business Enterprise, developing business plans and strategies, raising finance, and managing people and business performance.

Bernard and Julie enjoy walking, swimming, the theatre and eating out, as well as raising funds for charities and community projects. They have a son who is an architect and a daughter who is a solicitor, both working in London.

SHEILA HAYLES

After a childhood living at stately homes such as Castle Howard ("firmly downstairs, before anybody gets the wrong impression: my parents were in service"), Sheila arrived in Henley-on-Thames aged 13 and has lived in the area ever since.

Following a career in regional newspapers, a change of direction saw her working at local conference centres before starting Town & Country Conferences with husband Allan in 1981. The company has grown to become one of the leading venue-finding services in the UK and Europe, providing a free service to a variety of clients to locate and book all types of meetings, events and incentives, using anything from five-star hotels to training centres, country house hotels and stately homes.

Over the past 25 years, Sheila and Allan have visited most of the major regions and cities of the UK and Europe, and have gathered an encyclopaedic knowledge of the hotel, meeting and hospitality industry. In their spare time, they enjoy eating out, visiting art galleries and museums, antiques, history, reading and cooking.

DEBRA JARDINE

Following the completion of a law degree, Debra's career commenced in 1984 with a subsidiary of Lloyds Bank, working in the sales and marketing department of a corporate relocation company. It then took a slightly different course after one of her later employers decided to sell his relocation business and purchase a luxury hotel, and requested Debra to undertake the promotion and marketing.

In 2001, Debra formed her own company based in Clifton, near Banbury. The PDQ Partnership specialises in providing marketing services to businesses, with a particular emphasis on generating measurable results which increase the bottom line.

Debra lives near Deddington in North Oxfordshire and is married to Shaun, a local solicitor. She has two teenage daughters and enjoys shopping, eating out, hosting dinner parties, theatre and beating her husband at golf!

SHAUN JARDINE

Shaun is a Litigation Partner with Brethertons Solicitors in Banbury, as well as Chairman of the Banbury Business Breakfast Club, Oxfordshire's largest business networking operation, and of the North Oxfordshire Sporting Club.

Shaun and his business partner first set up in Banbury in 1991, after leaving a large Surrey solicitors firm. Brethertons is now one of the largest firms in the south Midlands, with offices in Banbury and Rugby, and employ over 120 people.

Married to Debra, Shaun spends his non-working hours eating out, playing golf, visiting the theatre/comedy clubs, and operating a teenage daughter taxi service.

TRACEY JEFFERIES

A passion for people was the driving force behind Tracey's desire to launch her own PR business, building on a background in retail management for John Lewis. Her skills were honed over the years with a realisation that PR was a growing industry calling for an intelligent approach, thereby dispelling the 'fluffy' image the industry had suffered from.

Langmans launched in February 2004, offering PR, marketing and event management, mainly for Oxfordshire-based clients. Success to date includes a programme of events for The Old Parsonage Hotel in Oxford, wine appreciation evenings so successful that they were immediately over-subscribed, and events aimed at educating local school children about food. Satisfying work also includes promoting Kuhnke Communication, a communication company who work with sportspeople such as James Cracknell, the Olympic gold medallist.

Re-married with a combined total of five children and two grandchildren, Tracey lives with her husband Paul in Longworth, near Kingston Bagpuize. Supporting Paul's second career as a musician, eating out and enjoying various local jazz events takes up any spare time.

TOM LEWIS

Tom has been General Manager at Le Manoir aux Quat' Saisons in Great Milton since February 2005. From the age of five, his interest in food started with cooking at home for his family. At 15, not even washing pots and dishes in a very ordinary hotel near home put Tom off his vocation into the hospitality industry.

His career in hotels formally started, after attaining management qualifications, at The Dorchester in Park Lane, as a trainee manager working in all the departments throughout the hotel. During his time at the Dorchester he was seconded to the Plaza Athenee in Paris and La Villa Magna Hotel in Madrid for a year. Tom then proceeded on his career working at Dukes Hotel in London, The Lygon Arms in Broadway as Deputy Manager, The Feathers Hotel in Woodstock as General Manager, and Great Fosters in Surrey as Hotel Manager, before joining Raymond Blanc at Le Manoir.

Married with two daughters, Tom and his wife Rosie live in Kirtlington. They both enjoy cooking, travelling and eating out.

SUZANNE LOCKHART

Suzanne joined Oxford City Council as Tourism Officer for Oxford in May 2004, where she has responsibility for management and promotion of tourism in the city. As the first fully-employed tourism officer for the council, she faces a challenging job of emphasising the importance of the tourism industry, the need for careful management, and influencing political views of the impact of tourism.

Originally from Glasgow, Suzanne began her career in 1996 in the planning department of Argyll & Bute Council, then moved to Edinburgh to become a Project Support Officer for Midlothian Council and then an Economic Development Officer for City of Edinburgh Council. In 2003, she was promoted to Senior Economic Development Officer in Edinburgh where she project-managed a major planning and visioning exercise with high profile representatives from over 50 key businesses across the city.

She has an MA in Geography from the University of Glasgow and a post-graduate MSc in Local Economic Development from Napier University, Edinburgh. She is also a member of the Tourism Management Institute.

Suzanne lives in Oxford with her partner Stuart. They enjoy eating-out, particularly seafood, and take regular trips back to Edinburgh to support the Scottish rugby team.

LINDA MOWAT

Linda is Senior Project Officer at the Pitt Rivers Museum in Oxford, overseeing the museum's unique collection of anthropological and archaeological artefacts.

ALISON PETRASH

Alison is Managing Director of Meet For Dinner, based in Witney. Alison was working at senior level for a large direct marketing company in 2002 when, during a chance conversation with a single 40-year old friend, they discussed how increasingly difficult it was to meet new, like-minded single people. The conversation got on to always feeling the odd one out when married friends held dinner parties, or going on mismatched blind-dates and internet dating disasters. Alison saw an opportunity to set up her own business meeting the needs of single people in the Oxfordshire area, and Meet For Dinner was born.

The company arranges meals out at a range of pubs, hotels and restaurants across Oxfordshire, for anywhere between 16 to 24 members at a time, as a way of introducing single people to each other. Individuals are invited to join if they are looking for new friends, are new to the area, or looking for a new partner.

BOB PRICE

Bob, who is the Lord Mayor of Oxford for the period 2005-2006, has lived in Oxford since 1976, and has been a City Councillor for 23 years, representing the Grandpont and New Hinksey areas of the city.

He did his undergraduate degree at Cambridge ("the other place"), and postgraduate studies at Warwick University, and now works as Director of Human Resources at Oxford Brookes University. He is an avid cyclist, walker and road and cross-country runner, having completed a quarter-century of marathons.

Married with two daughters, Bob and his wife Joanna enjoy the full range of cultural goodies on offer in Oxford, from the galleries and bookshops to the theatre, opera and live music, all in walking distance from their home in central Oxford.

MAX REINHARDT

Musician, writer, broadcaster and DJ, Max describes himself as being "at heart, a musical activist. The following list, which masquerades as my CV, reveals me as a promiscuous collaborator whose life revolves around music: writing it, playing it one way or another, writing and making radio programmes about it, finding new sources of it, and devising and creating new contexts for it."

He is: London Club DJ (Shrine, Radio Gagarin, Lizard), music writer (Straight No Chaser/Froots/S'Lines), compiler, radio presenter/contributor/music consultant (BBC World Service/In Flight/BBC Radio 2 & 3), DJ/co-MD of the Shrine Synchro System which tours internationally; programmer of international music festivals; and workshop leader/deviser for the London Jazz Festival, BBC Talent, BBC Blast and internationally for the British Council.

He is currently hard at work on Ketubah, a Litvak wedding installation; the Shrine Synchro System's Klezmaniax project for the Klezmapolitan festival in Paris; and a book about Fela Anikulapo Kuti, the creator of AfroBeat.

ANDREW RYAN

Andrew is Director of Oxford Castle Ltd, responsible for the regeneration of the Oxford Castle Heritage Project in the centre of the city, comprising the Malmaison Hotel together with eight restaurants, a cafe, 40 apartments, an art gallery, market trading and a heritage interpretation centre.

A registered architect, Andrew works for the Osborne Group, developers of the project. The company specialises in the re-use of historic buildings and is currently involved in the re-development of Buxton Spa in Derbyshire, with other projects in Bath and Bournemouth.

Andrew and his wife live in Henley-on-Thames.

CLARE SALTER

Clare is the Administrator of the Jacqueline du Pre Music Building at St Hilda's College, Oxford. She started her career in arts administration working for the Musician's Diary Service in Surrey, looking after the work diaries of professional musicians. Moving to Oxford in 2002, she joined Blackwells and then moved to the Jacqueline du Pre Music Building, looking after the day-to-day running of the venue.

Clare read Music & Philosophy at Manchester Metropolitan University, and in her spare time is an active fencer, competing at local and national level. She has also taken up karate and is currently spending her weekends walking the Pennine Way. Always a keen musician, she still finds time to play the cello and piano with friends.

YASMIN SIDHWA

Yasmin has worked as an actor, director and storyteller, and is currently Youth and Education Co-ordinator at Pegasus Theatre, and teaches drama at Oxford University in the Department of Educational Studies.

Graduating from Leeds University, Yasmin performed as Elmire in an adaptation of Moliere's Tartuffe for the National Theatre at the Cottesloe and Lyttelton Theatres, and on a two-year UK and international tour. She has toured in the US, and was a company member of both Tara Arts Group and Greenwich Young People's Theatre. She has also performed in repertory theatre, on television in Wycliffe and The Bill, and in many BBC4 radio plays.

As a director and storyteller, Yasmin has taken shows to the Edinburgh Festival, worked for the International Women's Festival in Oxford, and performed in and directed Jenny Lewis' Garden of the Senses at the 2005 Oxford Literary Festival

Yasmin has worked for many organisations in Oxfordshire using drama and theatre as her specialism, including Oxford Touring Theatre Company, Ithaca, Life Chance (a project with homeless young people), PEEP (Peers Early Education Partnership) and schools throughout Oxfordshire. She has directed many Youth Theatre productions for Pegasus Theatre, the most recent being Ben Coren's adaptation of Philip Pullman's I Was A Rat.

BRIAN SINFIELD

Brian is Managing Director of Brian Sinfield Gallery in Burford. He emigrated to Australia at 19 and spent much of his early life working with animals in zoos, before returning to the UK in 1964, helping to set up the Cotswold Zoological Society, which he ran as Director for several years. In 1972, he decided on a career change based on his passion for collecting paintings, and opened his first gallery at Stow-on-the-Wold, specialising in early English watercolours and Victorian paintings. Seven galleries later and now one of the longest-established galleries in the Cotswolds, he deals in leading 20th century and contemporary artists.

Brian lives in a large Victorian farmhouse near Burford with his wife Ann, a former teacher and great cook whose ambition it has always been to open a restaurant. Both like eating out at good restaurants, and travelling, whilst Brian also enjoys the more solitary pleasures of hill walking, fly fishing, reading and writing.

KATHRYN SMITH

Kathryn is Marketing Manager for Oxford Limited and the University of Oxford Shop. Following a degree in modern languages and a year spent working in translation for EDF in Paris, Kathryn moved to Oxford to take up a career in marketing.

She started work at The University of Oxford's own shop, running their successful mail order business and advertising campaigns, before moving to Oxford Limited, the parent company, to manage the marketing activities of the worldwide licensing programme. All profits from the company are endowed back to the University to fund its activities, and all merchandise and services must adhere to a strict ethical policy.

Kathryn is married to Andrew and they live in Summertown, north Oxford. She enjoys the variety that life in Oxford brings with its museums, art galleries and history, not forgetting fabulous cocktail bars and restaurants.

JILL TRELOGGEN

Jill is managing Director of Jill Treloggen Interiors in Witney, having spent most of her previous working life in sales and marketing roles. After gaining a degree in business at Oxford Brookes University, she worked for Marks & Spencer in buying, moving to an Oxford-based training company, before taking up a role as Business Development Director for a loyalty marketing company working with Tesco and Asda.

Throughout her career, Jill always had a passion for interior design, and studied for this whilst working, before deciding the time was right to set up her own interior design business. Today the business has three main focuses: working with property developers to furnish and stage show homes, working with many of the local letting agencies providing interior and furnishing packages, and providing interior design for private clients.

Jill lives in Witney with her husband Rod, and enjoys travelling, both abroad and in this country. They both love to sample new menus on their travels, and particularly enjoy Thai cuisine. On a recent trip to Thailand they undertook a Thai cookery course and can now wow their friends at dinner parties!

VICTORIA TURNER

Victoria enjoys a double role as Managing Director of Effective Personnel Solutions and Vitality Clinic, both based in Oxfordshire.

Having worked in sales and marketing for over 20 years, and latterly in recruitment consultancy, Victoria set up Effective Personnel Solutions, a recruitment consultancy sourcing staff across Oxfordshire and The Thames Valley in a variety of sectors, including executive, marketing, PR, events, publishing, sales, human resources, accountancy, commercial and graduates.

Victoria is a qualified stress consultant and life/career coach, and utilises NLP (Neuro-Linguistic Programming) in both areas. Vitality Clinic was therefore a natural progression, and whilst performing one-to-one consultations and workshops, also provides on-site treatments and workshops for company clients.

Victoria has a passion for literature, poetry, history and music, from country and blues to the classics, and a keen interest in all things holistic and spiritual.

RACHEL VINEY

Rachel is a communications consultant and writer, specialising in media and the arts. As well as working for the cultural development agency, Oxford Inspires, she is writing a book about the UK cultural sector. Rachel has lived in Wallingford for the past 14 years.

CLAIRE WILLCOX

Claire, who is Business Development Manager for Lloyds TSB in Oxfordshire, joined the company in 1988 at the main branch in Carfax, Oxford. She quickly discovered that it was business banking that took her fancy, and helped to set up one of the first business banking centres in Oxford in 1993. Since then, she has worked in and around the Oxford area as a business manager, until more recently taking up her current post, a role that involves meeting with both new clients and existing businesses, and also increasing Lloyds TSB's profile in the Oxfordshire area.

Claire is married with twin girls aged eight and lives in Witney. In her spare time she tries to go to the gym to work off all the business lunches. She also loves to discover new locations for holidays.

AMANDA WYATT

Amanda manages the City Centre Department of Knight Frank in Oxford, which sells quality townhouses and apartments throughout Oxford as well as family homes close to Oxford in Boars Hill. Amanda started working in the property business in 1998, attracted by the combination of working with people, creating marketing campaigns, and dealing with period property and historic architecture. Beautiful and historic homes have always been a fascination, and from a very early age she remembers enjoying sitting in the doctor's waiting room purely because they had so many back copies of Country Life.

Educated at Goldsmiths College, University of London and following on with an MA in Industrial Design at Central Saint Martins College of Art and Design, she went on to work in marketing before moving into property.

Having worked as a photographic assistant to a fine artist, which took her all over the world, her many interests include travel, fine art, design and writing.

Amanda is a farmer's daughter from north Oxfordshire and lives in Sibford Gower.

OUR YOUNGER CONTRIBUTORS...

Oxfordshire has some wonderful attractions for children as well as adults. Who better to ask about the best place to spend a day out in the county than our young Location Scouts, who know exactly what they like to do and what makes a good day out? With many thanks to: Alex Dolphin (age 8), the next David Attenborough? Leah Everton (age 10), the next Anna Ford? and Lucy Endacott (age 11) and her sister Hannah (age 13), maybe the next Nigella and Delia?

ALEX DOLPHIN

LEAH EVERTON

LUCY & HANNAH ENDACOTT

I'd like to thank my mum...

This book is the result of many months of eating, drinking and exploring. It's a tough job! It started as an idea over one too many bottles of wine, and ended up as a full-time job for both of us, and a journey that has tested the patience of our bank manager.

Has it been worth it? You be the judge. We certainly had fun. Along the way we met many people who have helped us achieve a dream to publish our own series of books. They are in no particular order, and if we have forgotten you, it was certainly not intentional: just blame it on a glass of Pinot Noir too many.

To the whole team who helped make this book possible. From Terry Causer who started the ball rolling with some serious brainstorming, to Steve Smith and Jon Booth from Domino Design Solutions who believed in our idea, and helped us to make it look fabulous. To Dan Prescott and Paul Watkins at Purple Turtle for the website, Steve Palmer at WACE, our printers, for helping us understand the joys of bookbinding, George and Shirley at Book Systems Plus for helping us to understand the wonderful world of book distribution, David Atkinson for his superb map, and Mark Bassett our photographer for putting up with our crazy ideas on how to take pictures. Thanks also to Matthew Millard Beer and Kate Oyler at Fleishman-Hillard, our PR people in London, for coming up with a great campaign and helping us create the full story of Classic Locations. A special mention to Rebecca Dawes who chose to spend the summer with us doing her work experience from college. Will she still want to be a journalist?

Thank you to Victoria Moon, Suzanne Lockhart and Kathelene Weiss for believing in the project from day one, and offering good advice and positive feedback. Thank you to every restaurant, hotel, shop and attraction we have featured in the book for being good enough to write about, and for keeping standards high.

To long term friends Michael & Brenda and John & Christina: we know you think we are mad, but thank you for your support along the way. It means everything to us.

From Kate: a big thank you to Mum. She allowed me to do my own thing, to make mistakes, but always to realise that there would be a next time, and that next time there would be a way to do it better. (Sorry, but I've always wanted to write that in a book!!)

Paul & Kate Rouse

Oxfordshire, October 2005.

Index: Oxford

Index: North Oxfordshire

Index: South Oxfordshire

Index: West Oxfordshire

Index: Eat

Index: Sleep

Index: Shop

Index: Visit

Index: A-Z

Index: A-Z

Index: Destinations

CLASSIC
LOCATiONS

OXFORDSHIRE

The inspiration for this book came from our travels overseas, and a mission to follow the locals: an excellent rule of thumb being that they always know the best places to eat, sleep, shop and visit.

Classic Locations gives visitors to Oxfordshire a chance to discover its favourite places and hidden secrets: places to enjoy, relax and experience the best that the wonderful city of Oxford and the surrounding county has to offer.

FAVOURiTE PLACES HiDDEN SECRETS AND HOW TO ENJOY THEM

BY PAUL ROUSE & KATE ROUSE

THE SMALL PRINT

First published in the United Kingdom in 2005 by Classic Locations Limited.

Any copy of this book issued by the publisher is sold subject to the condition that it shall not, by way of trade or otherwise, be lent, re-sold, hired out or otherwise circulated, without the publisher's prior consent, in any form of binding or cover other than that in which it is published.

© 2005 Classic Locations Limited

Classic Locations Limited Reg. No. 4694287

www.classiclocations.com

All rights reserved. No part of this publication may be reproduced or transmitted in any form or by any means, electronic or mechanical, including photocopy, recording or any information storage or retrieval system, without permission in writing from the publisher.

Every effort has been made to ensure the information in this book is correct. However, the publishers cannot accept liability for any errors or omissions. Every effort has been made to trace and contact the copyright holders of all materials in the book.

The rights of Paul Rouse and Kate Rouse to be identified as the authors of this work have been asserted in accordance with the Copyright, Designs and Patents Act 1988.

Original photography by Mark Bassett at The Source Photography

Map illustration by David Atkinson

Designed by Domino Design Solutions

Printed and bound in Great Britain by WACE, Swindon

Cataloguing in Publication Data is available from the British Library.

ISBN 0-9550880-0-3